HOW TO
CRAFT WITH PAPER

WITH OVER 50 TECHNIQUES AND 20 EASY PROJECTS

PAVILION

Contents

Get stuck in!

Paper. It's often our first crafty love. We graduate from scribbling all over it, gluing glitter across it and folding it into aeroplanes to developing a life-long appreciation for stunning stationery, stickers and beautifully-finished prints. It's tactile, malleable and versatile – we'll show you on these pretty pages how you can use this civilisation-building material to make everything from jewellery to lampshades.

The techniques open to you when you're working with paper are vast and we've covered a huge selection here, from origami to scrapbooking, cardmaking to stamping. You'll also find papier mâché, quilling, paper-cutting and stitching being used to create beautiful, modern pieces you can give as gifts or keep for yourself. Far from flimsy and solely decorative, let our designers demonstrate how paper can be durable, strong and practical too.

Turn the page to get started and be surprised at what you can create with sheets, leaves and strips!

Lara

Lara Watson
Editor, *Mollie Makes*

Projects

Cut and fold card collection

Get to grips with basic cutting, scoring and folding techniques to make this simple set of dimensional greetings cards. The designs are adaptable to suit just about any occasion, and you can also customise colours and patterns, or add a message, so each finished card is perfectly tailored to the recipient.

MATERIALS

Sheets of thin card

Plain and patterned papers

Adhesives: foam mounting pads, glue stick and PVA glue

Craft knife, cutting mat and metal ruler

Scissors, ruler and pencil

Bone folder (optional)

Corner-rounder punch (optional)

SIZE

Heart card: 10 x 10cm (4 x 4in)
Apple card: 12.5 x 11cm (4⅞ x 4¼in)
Star card: 11 x 11cm (4¼ x 4¼in)
Bow card: 8.5 x 11cm (3⅞ x 4¼in)
Flower card: 9 x 13cm (3½ x 5in)
Stag card: 10 x 12cm (4 x 4¾in)

FEATURED TECHNIQUES

- Transferring templates (p. 104)
- Scoring and folding (p. 108)
- Using a craft knife (p. 106)

BEFORE YOU BEGIN

To make the apple card, a double-sided sheet of patterned card is required. If you don't have anything suitable in your paper stash, you can simply stick two contrasting sheets of paper together, back to back.

If you don't have a corner-rounder punch, use a small coin to round off the corners of the base cards: place the coin in each corner in turn, draw around it with a pencil, then cut around the marked curves.

KIRSTY NEALE

Kirsty is a designer-maker and author based in London. She enjoys working with fabric, paper, pattern and illustration, and she is very detail-focussed (which is just a nice way of saying obsessive). She has written several craft books and blogs at www.kirstyneale.co.uk

METHOD: HEART CARD

{01} Prepare and decorate base card
Cut a 21 x 10.5cm (8¼ x 4⅛in) piece of card and fold it in half. Cover the card front with patterned paper. With the folded edge at the top, add a strip of plain paper along the bottom edge of the card front. Round the corners.

{02} Prepare the heart motif
Copy the heart template (p. 134) onto two contrasting pieces of paper and cut out. Score and fold along the centre of each heart as marked by the dotted line. Using a toothpick, spread a thin line of PVA glue along the creased fold at the back of one of the hearts. Press the heart glue-side down on top of the second heart, taking care to line up the folds. Allow the glue to dry for a few minutes before proceeding with step 3.

{03} Finish the card
Working on the back of your joined hearts, apply a thin line of glue to the creased fold and then press the joined heart motif glue-side down onto the centre front of the base card. When the glue is completely dry, gently fold the sides of each heart upwards, away from the background, to create a simple but effective 3D look.

METHOD: APPLE CARD

{01} Prepare base card
Cut a 22 x 12.5cm (8⅝ x 4⅞in) piece of double-sided card and fold it in half. Round the corners.

{02} Prepare the apple motif
With the folded edge at the left-hand side, measure the halfway point along the top edge of the base card and lightly mark the vertical with a pencil. Copy the apple template (p. 134) onto the card front in pencil, aligning the straight edge of the template with the marked vertical line and positioning it approximately 2cm (¾in) from the bottom edge of the base card.

Open out the base card and, following the template markings, use a craft knife to carefully cut along each of the solid lines on the marked apple design. Score along the dotted centre line, then fold over the two shaded sections (see template). Refold the base card.

{03} Finish the card
Working on the card front, stick a contrasting piece of paper behind the apple cut-out. Copy the stalk template onto brown paper and cut out. Glue the stalk to the top of the apple.

Note

For a fun Christmas card, cut a nose from red paper and mount Rudolph onto a festive print background paper. You could also use alphabet stickers or a printed sentiment to add a greeting to the front (or inside) of your finished cards.

METHOD: STAR CARD

{01} Prepare and decorate base card
Cut a 22 x 11cm (8½ x 4¼in) piece of card and fold it in half to give you your base card.

Cut a contrasting piece of card 10cm (4in) square, and round the corners. Cut two narrow strips of card 7.5cm (3in) tall; glue one strip behind each side edge of the contrasting card square. Fix this panel to the front of the base card using foam mounting pads.

{02} Prepare the star motif
Copy the star template (p. 134) onto thin, patterned card, and cut out. Score along the dotted lines as marked on the template. Fold the score lines: the folds going out to each point should be mountain folds (pointing upwards), and those in-between should be valley folds (pointing downwards).

{03} Finish the card
Place two tiny foam mounting pads under each point of the star, then carefully press down the star into position on the front of the card.

METHOD: BOW CARD

{01} Prepare and decorate base card
Cut a 20 x 11cm (8 x 4¼in) piece of card and fold it in half to give you your base card. Cut a piece of paper in a contrasting colour slightly smaller than the base card; round the corners and glue it to the front of the card.

{02} Prepare the bow motif
Copy the bow template (p. 134) onto your chosen paper and cut out. Score and fold along the dotted lines as marked.

To form the bow shape, use a little glue to stick the folded sections together, matching the letters on the template (A to A, B to B, etc.). Cut a 0.8 x 2.5cm (⁵⁄₁₆ x 1in) paper strip and glue it around the centre of the bow. Use the tail template to cut out two tail pieces from your paper, then glue them in place to the back of the bow.

{03} Finish the card
Stick the completed bow to the front of the card.

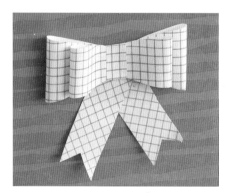

METHOD: FLOWER CARD

{01} Prepare and decorate base card
Cut a 27 x 9.5cm (10½ x 3¾in) piece of card and fold it in half to give you your base card. Cut a 3cm (1⅛in) strip of patterned paper and glue it to the bottom edge of the folded card. Round the corners.

{02} Prepare the flower motifs
To make each blossom, cut out the two flower templates (one small, one large) (p. 135) from your chosen papers, making sure to cut along the solid line between petals A and B. Score and fold along all of the dotted lines.

Working on each flower in turn, spread glue over the front of petal A and stick it to the back of petal B. This turns the flat paper shape into a three-dimensional, cup-shaped flower. Glue the small flowers inside the larger ones.

{03} Finish the card
Copy the stem templates (p. 135) onto paper or thin card and cut out. Glue the stems to the front of the card, taking care to position them far enough apart that there is room to add a flower at the top of each one.

Mollie MAKES HOW TO CRAFT WITH PAPER

METHOD: STAG CARD

{01} Prepare and decorate base card
Cut a 24 x 10cm (9½ x 4in) piece of card and fold it in half to give you your base card. Cut a piece of paper in a contrasting colour slightly smaller than the base card; round the corners and attach it to the front of the base card using foam mounting pads. Round the corners of the base card.

{02} Prepare the stag head motif
Copy the three stag head templates (A, B and C) (p. 135) onto a tan-coloured patterned paper and cut out. Score along the marked dotted lines to fold each piece in half vertically.

Spread glue over the back of piece A. Stick the left-hand side of piece B to the right-hand side of piece A, and the right-hand side of piece C to the left-hand side of piece A.

{03} Finish the card
Spread glue over the backs of the remaining (shaded) areas of pieces B and C, and press the assembled stag head into place on the card front.

Cut out the eyes and nose from black paper, and stick into place on the stag's face.

Papercraft Story
When card-making, I spend ages sketching, choosing colours and patterns, cutting pieces out and moving them around. It always involves a lot of standing back and squinting to get a better idea of the overall look. Some days I worry I'll get extra wrinkles caused by the 'card-maker's squint'. But, just like laughter lines, I figure that the fun I have earning them makes them worthwhile in the end! *Kirsty Neale*

Wise owl bowls

Make an eye-catching bowl with the simplest of papier mâché techniques resurrected from your earliest school days. Layers of paper are simply formed around a balloon form. The how-to may be child's play but the end result is a design-interior gem. The result is so good, you'll want to make two!

MATERIALS

Paper for layering: newspaper, and plain newsprint or thin plain paper

Paper for decorating: patterned tissue paper or decoupage paper

Small piece of thin card

Balloon and plastic cup

PVA glue, water and brush

Small scissors and craft knife

Tape: masking and sticky tape

Acrylic paints and selection of small paintbrushes

Matt varnish

SIZE

Approx. 18 x 17cm (7 x 6¾in)

FEATURED TECHNIQUES

- Transferring templates (p. 104)
- Papier mâché: Layering (p. 128)

BEFORE YOU BEGIN

The papier mâché is applied in alternating layers of newspaper and plain newsprint so that it is easy to see when one layer has been completed. Prepare your papers in advance, tearing them into small pieces measuring approximately 5cm (2in) square; keep your newspaper pile separate from your newsprint pile.

Papercraft Story

I thought the simple technique of making a bowl over a balloon form could be made more interesting by turning the finished result into an owl. I love owl motifs and have combined simple shapes, patterned paper and pastels to create this adorable pair of designs. *Jaina Minton*

METHOD

{01} Papier mâché the balloon

Take a balloon and inflate it to the diameter size you desire for the finished bowl; tie a knot in the end of the balloon. Place the inflated balloon knot end down inside a plastic cup or other suitable container and secure it in place with masking tape. This will keep the balloon upright and balanced as you apply the layers of papier mâché.

Papier mâché a layer of your newspaper pieces onto the balloon, pasting them on with a brush using a mixture of PVA and water (4 parts glue to 1 part water). Overlap all edges and paste the glue mix on top of each piece as well. Allow the first layer to dry completely, then apply a layer of plain newsprint pieces. Once that layer has dried, apply two more layers, one newspaper and one newsprint, allowing each layer to dry before applying the next. Four layers should be sufficient to ensure a solid, sturdy bowl, but if you do decide to add more, make sure the last layer is a plain layer so it is ready to paint onto.

{02} Remove the balloon

Allow the final layer of papier mâché to dry thoroughly, then remove the balloon from the cup it is sitting in. Snip the balloon to pop it and safely discard the balloon. You are now left with a bowl shape with a ragged edge. Deciding how deep you want your bowl to be, draw a line under the ragged edge all the way around. Trim along this line with scissors or a craft knife to neaten.

Use the owl ear template (p. 138) to mark and cut out two ears from thin card. Aligning the dotted line to the rim of the bowl, attach one ear to each side of the owl's head, securing it in place with tape. Papier mâché some more newspaper onto the ears to ensure they are as secure and sturdy as the bowl itself, allowing layers to dry in between.

JAINA MINTON

Designer-maker Jaina Minton creates cheerful, quirky pieces to adorn the home. Working from her studio in Kent she is surrounded, almost buried, under her huge collection of colourful papers and rolls of spare sticky tape. She enjoys sharing her process, along with DIY makes, on her blog www.jainamadethis.com. Further work and her online shop can be found at www.polkadotsundays.com

{01}

{02}

{03} Decorate the exterior

Once the ears have dried, use white acrylic paint to block out the main shapes for the owl design, marking on large circles for the eyes and an upside-down triangle for the forehead (a).

Use light grey paint to paint all over the exterior of the bowl, leaving just the blocked-out areas unpainted. Mix up some pastel colours and paint within your guide shapes to create the broad features of the owl (b).

You are now ready to add the patterned paper layer. For the owl's forehead area, cut strips of patterned tissue or decoupage paper and glue on following the photo as your guide; trim off any paper that extends beyond the rim. Use the feather templates (p. 138) to cut feathers from your patterned papers. For the top row of feathers, use feather shape 1, trimming as necessary to align your cut feathers with your owl's eye mask shape, then glue the remaining rows of feather shape 2 in place so that the feathers interlock. Cut circles for the owl's pupils and thin, long triangles of paper to radiate out from each pupil. Glue on a paper triangle between the owl's eyes for the beak (c).

{03a}

{03b}

{03c}

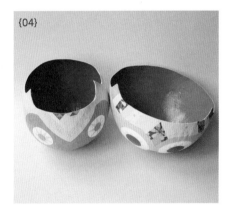
{04}

{04} Paint the interior and finish

Once the paper decoration is complete, leave to dry completely. Once the paper is dry, paint the inside of your completed owl bowl in a bright, contrasting colour. Once the paint is dry, varnish to finish.

Note

Choose your embellishing colours: select a limited colour palette to keep the design from becoming childish. Pastels with a bright interior have been chosen here, but if you prefer, try white with a gold interior.

Lily fairy lights

If you thought that only specialised origami paper can be used for folding origami, think again. This string of origami lilies, pretty garland by day and illuminating fairy lights by night, make good use of recycled papers. Book pages and music paper sheets have been used, but old maps, magazines and wrapping papers work just as well.

MATERIALS

10 sheets of lightweight paper approx. 13.5 x 13.5cm (5¼ x 5¼in)

LED light string with 10 bulbs

Paper trimmer

Hot glue gun

Scissors

SIZE

Light string approx. 1.25m (1½yd) length; each lily approx. 8cm (3⅛in) long

FEATURED TECHNIQUES

• Origami (p. 118)

BEFORE YOU BEGIN

Choose paper that is 80–100gsm – about the weight of regular printer paper. Cut your paper to size using a paper trimmer following the dimension markings for accurate cutting.

Practise folding the origami lilies on regular printer paper cut to size, following the Fold an Origami Lily Flower instructions on p. 18. Once you have achieved lilies you are happy with, you can move on to fold your final 10 flowers from your selected papers.

It is very important to use an LED light string which has bulbs that remain cool and safe for paper shades. Do be sure to test that all the bulbs are working first, before gluing your origami flowers in place.

MEI LIANG

Caimei Liang, or Mei for short, is the owner of and designer for Mei origami studio. Mei rediscovered origami, her childhood hobby, when working as a part-time babysitter when a student, and hasn't looked back since. To get to know more about Mei origami studio, follow her Facebook page or her online shop www.meiorigami.etsy.com

Papercraft Story

I love origami and I also care about the environment, so I try my best to re-use papers for my origami projects, such as pages from unwanted or damaged books and out-of-date maps. The more I fold, the more I realise how a simple sheet of paper can turn into an amazing object that will brighten up the world. *Mei Liang*

FOLD AN ORIGAMI LILY FLOWER

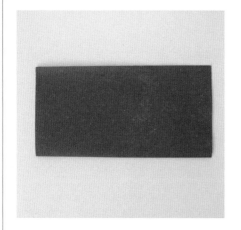

{01} Fold a square of paper in half.

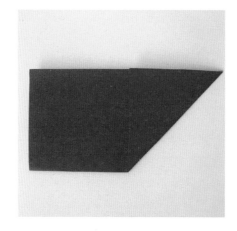

{02} Fold one corner up diagonally.

{03} Turn the paper over and fold the other corner up diagonally.

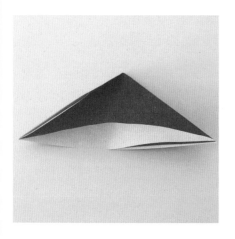

{04} Rotate the triangle so that the open ends are facing you.

{05} Open it up on one side to the maximum and flatten it to form a square base. Rotate the open side to the top. There are now four sides to your unit.

{06} Fold one side to the centre line then unfold to create the crease.

{07} Open the top left-hand side from the inside and flatten it as shown.

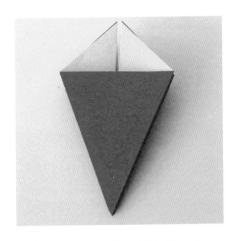

{08} Repeat steps 6 and 7 to the other three sides. There should now be eight sides to your unit.

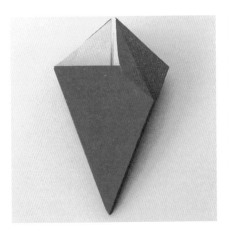

{09} Fold the top right-hand side down to the centre line.

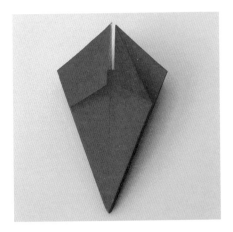

{10} Now repeat step 9 on the left-hand side.

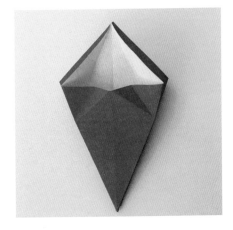

{11} Unfold each side. Open it from the inside and pull the paper down.

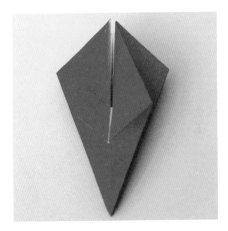

{12} This creates a triangle at the bottom edge as shown.

{13} Fold the triangle up.

{14} Repeat steps 9–13 on the remaining faces of the unit.

{15} Turn the unit to look like the photo.

{16} Fold the right-hand side inwards to the centre line.

{17} Repeat on the left-hand side.

{18} Repeat steps 16 and 17 to the remaining faces of the unit.

{19} Fold one petal down.

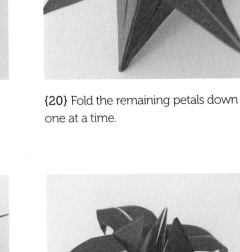

{20} Fold the remaining petals down one at a time.

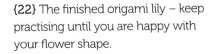

{21} Use a pen to curve the petals.

{22} The finished origami lily – keep practising until you are happy with your flower shape.

METHOD

{01} Fold 10 origami lily flowers

Once you have perfected your lily folding, fold 10 origami lilies, five using music paper sheets and five using book pages.

{02} Attach the lilies to the LED light string

Snip off the bottom of each lily to create a small hole for the light bulb to go through. Put the light bulb through the hole and apply a little hot glue to the bottom of the light bulb, then quickly pull the light bulb down into the lily.

When you are happy with the position of the light bulb inside the lily, give it a little squeeze where the hot glue is: this helps to spread the hot glue evenly and will ensure that the light bulb attaches better for a nice, clean finish.

{02}

Stitched photo napkin rings

Add a personal touch to your party table with these photo napkin rings. Pick out your guest's face, even in a group photo, by embroidering the simple heart motif in running stitch or backstitch. Break the ice with funny snaps, or ask your guests for a baby photo, or remind them of 'that time when...'. What's one embarrassing photo between friends?

MATERIALS

Digital photo of each guest, ideally a great head shot

A4 sheets of 160gsm white cardstock

Size 5 milliner's needle (also known as a straw needle)

Stranded cotton embroidery threads in various colours

Ruler, pencil and eraser

Scissors: paper and embroidery

SIZE

17cm (6¾in) wide x 5cm (2in) high

FEATURED TECHNIQUES

- Transferring templates (p. 104)
- Stitching (p. 117)

BEFORE YOU BEGIN

Prepare your photographs in advance. On a computer, open the photos you have chosen in a picture editor or insert them into word processing software. Crop or resize each photo so that it is roughly 5cm (2in) tall (don't worry about the width) and clearly shows your guest's face. Centre each photo to print in the middle of an A4 sheet, and print the photos in black and white (or grayscale) onto cardstock.

Papercraft Story

At weekends I love to visit postcard fairs where I'll spend hours leafing through vintage picture postcards. I've combined my love of old pictures with my love of embroidery to launch a range of hand-stitched prints – the inspiration behind this project. By turning all your photos black and white, they'll sit better together at the table and really make your coloured thread pop. My advice is to be bold with your colour choices: here, a little neon thread makes a big impact.

Genevieve Brading

METHOD

{01} Cut napkin ring template

Draw a 17 x 5cm (6¾ x 2in) rectangle around each of your printed photos, with the photo in the middle. To create the end slots, draw a straight line 1cm (⅜in) away from the short side edges, from bottom to middle on one side and from top to middle on the other. Cut out each napkin ring along your marked lines (including the slot lines). Rub out any visible pencil marks.

{02} Prepare napkin rings for stitching

Make a tracing of the heart motif (p. 138). Use a little bit of washi tape or a paperclip to attach the traced design to one of your prepared napkin ring templates, making sure the heart is centered around your guest's face.

Poke your unthreaded needle along the heart design at 2–3mm (⅛in) intervals, from front to back through both layers of paper. Remove the tracing paper.

{03} Stitch the heart motifs

Stranded cotton embroidery thread is made up of six strands. Separate two strands and thread these together in your needle. Embroider the holes in backstitch (as is being shown in the photo) or running stitch. Secure the thread tails on the back of the napkin ring by weaving them through some stitches.

{04} Finish the napkin rings

To form the napkin ring, bring the ends together and slot in place.

{01}

{02}

{03}

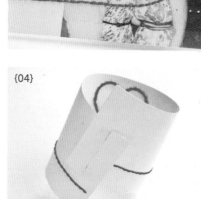

{04}

GENEVIEVE BRADING
OF FLOSS & MISCHIEF

Genevieve loves putting a modern twist on needlework. As the designer-maker behind needlework business Floss & Mischief, she hand-embroiders photos, and designs modern cross-stitch patterns, to get people stitching. When Genevieve's not embroidering, you'll find her dancing like no-one's watching at Mischief HQ. Buy her patterns, kits and stitched art at www.flossandmischief.com

Cut and close flower boxes

Two paper boxes in sweet pastel shades, one with a square base and one hexagonal, both perfect for presenting little gifts, especially jewellery. Each is topped with a 3D flower closure and decorated with metallic confetti-style polka dots. So, if you want to fine-tune your paper shaping and sculpting skills, this is the perfect project for you.

MATERIALS

A3 sheets of 135gsm paper: one each of pale pink and pale mint

A5 sheets of 135gsm paper: one each of medium pink, medium mint and gold

Craft knife, cutting mat and metal ruler

Scissors

Bone folder and embossing tool

Adhesives: tacky and glue stick

Circle craft punch, 1.5mm (optional)

SIZE

Square box:
8 x 8 x 10.5cm (3⅛ x 3⅛ x 4⅛in)

Hexagonal box:
11.5 x 10 x 8cm (4½ x 4 x 3⅛in)

FEATURED TECHNIQUES

- Transferring templates (p. 104)
- Using a craft knife (p. 106)
- Scoring and folding (p. 108)
- Paper manipulation: Curling (p. 110)

Papercraft Story

For me, paper is the most versatile, readily available, playful and satisfying of materials. It can be cut and delicate, embossed and luxurious, or folded and rigid. My fascination with paper is long-standing and some of my earliest childhood memories involve making origami penguins, paper snowflakes and paper doll chains. *Sarah Matthews*

METHOD: HEXAGONAL BOX

{01} Cut the box template
Enlarge the hexagonal box template (p. 137) and use to cut out the hexagonal box base from your A3 sheet of pale mint paper. Use an embossing tool and ruler to score along the dotted/dashed lines, then use a bone folder to fold along your scored lines to create mountain or valley folds as marked on the template.

{02} Cut out the petals and stamens
Use the petal template (p. 137) to cut six petals from medium mint paper and the stamen template (p. 137) to cut six stamens from gold paper.

{03} Sculpt the petals
Take a cylindrical object such as a smooth pencil and roll the end of each petal attached to the box backwards around it, stopping around half way down the petal, then curl the base of the petal forwards around the pencil to shape it. Repeat to shape the individually cut petals.

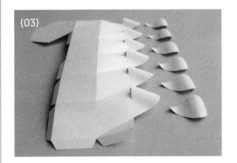

{04} Attach individual petals to box
Take one individual petal and apply a little tacky glue to the back of the pointed end. Stick it onto the box to lie opposite an attached petal as illustrated in the photo and repeat to attach each of the petals in place.

Apply tacky glue to the back of the pointed end of the gold stamens. Stick a stamen onto the inner corner of each attached petal, then pull each stamen upwards to crease it at the base.

{05} Assemble the box
Apply tacky glue to the front of the right-hand side tab and attach to the back of the left-hand edge. Fold the five base tabs so they are at a right angle to the sides; apply tacky glue to the bottom of the tabs and then press the base hexagon down onto the tabs.

To close the top of the box, twist the top of the box inwards allowing the creases to fall into place, then use your finger to gently press down in the centre of the flower.

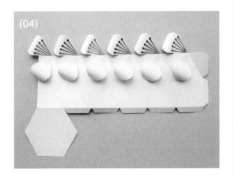

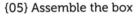

METHOD: SQUARE BOX

{01} Cut the box template

Enlarge the square box template (p. 136) and use to cut out the square box base from your A3 sheet of pale pink paper. Use an embossing tool and ruler to score along the dotted lines, then, using a bone folder, fold to create mountain or valley folds as marked on the template.

{02} Cut out the petals and stamens

Use the petal template (p. 136) to cut two from medium pink paper and the stamen template (p. 136) to cut two from gold paper.

{03} Decorate the square box base

Use your circular craft punch to cut your polka dots from the gold paper, then stick in place randomly over the central strip of the square box base, which will become the sides of the box. Trim off the edge of any dots overlapping at the top or bottom of the strip.

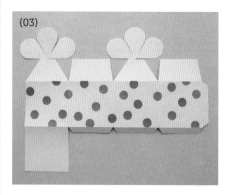

{03}

{04} Sculpt the petals

Take a cylindrical object such as a smooth pencil and roll the end of each petal attached to the box backwards around it, stopping around half way down the petal, then curl the base of the petal forwards around the pencil to shape it. Repeat to shape the petals of the medium pink cut petal pieces.

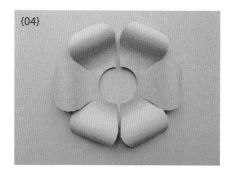

{04}

{05} Prepare cut petal pieces to attach to box

Apply a line of tacky glue along the inner edge of the first two petals only on the reverse of each of your cut petal pieces.

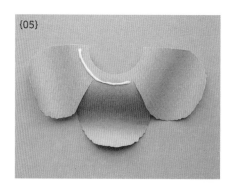

{05}

{06} Attach cut petal pieces to box

Take one of your prepared cut petal pieces and stick it below the first group of attached petals on the box, positioning it so that the right edge of the dark pink petal piece touches the right edge of the pale pink piece

SARAH MATTHEWS

Sarah creates paper-cut stationery, decorations, artwork and bespoke wedding products, exploring cutting, folding, slotting and interlocking to create innovative and fun paper surfaces and forms. Much of her work is pattern-based, taking inspiration from the shape and repetition she sees in architecture and nature to create fun geometric and botanical designs with flashes of playful, bright pastels and metallics. To see more of her work visit www.sarahlouisematthews.co.uk

below the slit: the left petal (the one with no glue) should be slotted underneath the pale pink flower petals, so that the left pale pink petal comes half way along the dark pink petal (see photo).

Working on the reverse, pull back the unattached dark pink petal, apply a dot of tacky glue to it spread out slightly with a scrap of card, then press it down onto the pale pink to secure.

Repeat steps 4–6 to complete the second flower.

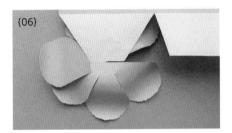

{06}

{07} Attach stamens to flowers

Working on the two gold stamen halves, fold the stamens upwards, creasing them at the base. Use tacky glue to stick each onto the centre of the pale pink half of each flower, aligning them with the top of the slit.

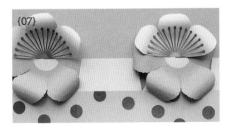

{07}

{08} Assemble the box

Apply tacky glue to the front of the right-hand side tab and attach to the back of the left-hand edge. Fold the three base tabs so they are at a right angle to the sides; apply tacky glue to the bottom of the tabs and then press the base square down onto the tabs.

{08}

Autumn garland

Paper-sculpted pumpkins, flowers and leaves decorate this seasonal wreath. The rich tones of the metallic papers contrast beautifully with the thick creamy letter-printed papers from recycled book pages. Made for autumn, the look can easily be changed to suit the season – for example, for a spring garland you could change the pumpkins to Easter eggs and use pretty pastels.

MATERIALS

One sheet of 35 x 35cm (13¾ x 13¾in) foam-core board

One sheet of 35 x 35cm (13¾ x 13¾in) grey paper for background

Selection of metallic papers: copper and silver patterned

One A4 sheet of thin card

Recycled book pages

Florists' wire

Adhesives: PVA glue and glue stick

Craft knife, cutting mat and metal ruler

Pencil and compass

Awl

Scissors, wire cutters and small pliers

SIZE

37cm (14½in) diameter

FEATURED TECHNIQUES

- Transferring templates (p. 104)
- Scoring and folding (p. 108)
- Paper manipulation: Fringing (p. 110)

Papercraft Story

As a child, my favourite activity at Christmas time was cutting paper-folded snowflakes. Today I am lucky enough to craft as a full-time career. Paper is the most versatile of all materials and its possibilities never cease to amaze me. I wanted to design a project to give new life to a damaged book. Many thousands of books are pulped each year, yet it is possible to create a thing of beauty from something that was destined for the recycling bin. **Clare Youngs**

METHOD

{01} Make the backing ring

Stick the sheet of grey paper to the foam-core board using glue. Use the compass to draw a circle with a radius of 16.5cm (6½in) onto the covered board (for a circle with a 33cm/13in diameter). Draw another circle 6cm (2⅜in) in from the first. Cut out using a craft knife and a cutting mat to give you your ring shape.

{02} Make the five-petalled flowers

Tracing off the large and small flower templates on p. 139, transfer the designs onto your recycled book pages. You will need approx 15 flowers in total. Cut out the flowers. Use a craft knife to cut along the marked centre lines and fold each back to stand upright to create the stamens in the centre of your flower. Working on each petal in turn, pinch the petal between your fingers to make a crease down its centre to give you a slightly cupped flower.

{02}

{03} Make the fringed flowers

Cut a strip of recycled book paper measuring 19 x 5cm (7⅝ x 2in). Fringe along its length: make your cuts approximately 2–3mm (⅛in) apart and stop cutting about 1cm (⅜in) from the bottom edge.

Cut a piece of metallic paper measuring 2 x 5cm (¾ x 2in) and fringe in the same way. Run a thin line of glue along the uncut edge of the recycled book paper strip. Place the fringed metallic strip at one end and tightly roll up from the metallic paper end. Ruffle up the fringed paper and curl outwards to finish the flower.

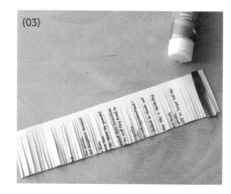
{03}

{04} Make the leaves

Use the leaf templates on p. 139 to mark out leaves in varying sizes onto your metallic and patterned papers – you will need approximately 20–25 in total. Cut out the leaves.

To shape the leaves, score down the centre of each leaf from top to bottom: use the tip of the craft knife blade only making sure that it just breaks the surface of the paper. Crease along the score lines.

{05} Make the pumpkins

Cover one side of the thin card with patterned paper. Cut 32 strips measuring 1 x 12cm (⅜ x 4¾in) from the covered card. Separate the strips into two piles of 16 strips and stack each pile so that the patterned side

CLARE YOUNGS

After working as a graphic designer and illustrator for a number of years, Clare turned to craft full time five years ago and she has not looked back since. She spends her day doing what she loves best – snipping, sewing, designing and making things. Catch up with her crafty way of life on her blog at www.clareyoungs.co.uk.

of the strips are uppermost. Working on each stacked pile at a time, use the awl to pierce a hole through the strips at both top and bottom, centring the holes 5mm (¼in) from the edge (a).

Cut a piece of wire measuring 11cm (4½in). Use pliers to bend over 5mm (¼in) of wire at the end, then bend it over again to make a 'knot'. Thread the unbent end of the wire through your stacked strips, making sure to thread it through from the patterned side of the card and pulling it through to the knot (b).

Now thread the wire through the holes at the bottom of the strips, this time taking it through the undecorated side first. Begin to curve the strips around to make a semicircle (c). Making sure that the wire measures approximately 5–6cm (2–2⅜in) from top to bottom of the pumpkin, use the pliers to fold over the wire a couple of times just beneath the pumpkin, then cut off the excess length. Continue to pull the card strips around to make the circle shape of the pumpkin.

To cover the wire at the top of the pumpkins, use the stalk template on p. 139 to cut two from the remains of the paper-covered card. Fold each stalk shape in half and stick in place (d).

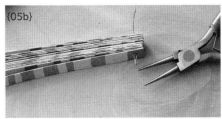

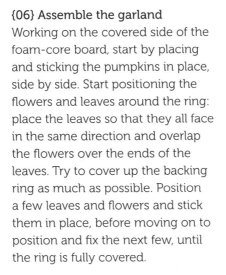

{06} Assemble the garland

Working on the covered side of the foam-core board, start by placing and sticking the pumpkins in place, side by side. Start positioning the flowers and leaves around the ring: place the leaves so that they all face in the same direction and overlap the flowers over the ends of the leaves. Try to cover up the backing ring as much as possible. Position a few leaves and flowers and stick them in place, before moving on to position and fix the next few, until the ring is fully covered.

Note

A recycled book garland makes a lovely decoration for a child's bedroom and is a great way to use pages from much-loved books that have started to fall apart from over-handling. Coloured illustrations are ideal for the flowers, bringing bright pops of colour to the design, and keeping the story alive.

Papier mâché cloud shelf

Brighten your walls with a decorative cloud shelf. The cloud appears to float across the room, scattering a shower of colourful raindrops. Manipulated from thick corrugated card and decorated with layers of papier mâché for strength, the shelf is strong enough to hold small objects for display.

MATERIALS

One sheet of A2 thick 2-ply (double-layer) corrugated card

Thin single-layer corrugated card (2m/2⅛yd of 8cm/3⅛in wide strips is required)

One sheet of A4 thin craft card

Newspaper

Adhesives: PVA glue, superglue and sticky tape

Acrylic paints and paintbrush

Thread

Picture hanging plate

Craft knife, cutting mat and metal ruler

Measuring tape

Scissors

SIZE

Approx. 65cm (25½in) wide x 50cm (20in) high (excluding raindrops) x 8cm (3⅛in) deep

FEATURED TECHNIQUES

- Transferring templates (p. 104)
- Papier mâché: Moulds and armatures (p. 127)

BEFORE YOU BEGIN

Cut thin, single-layer corrugated card into strips measuring 8cm/3⅛in wide. The strips will be cut into smaller pieces to match the curves of the cloud and the longest piece will need to be approximately 55cm (22in) for the base of the cloud. It is important to make sure that the lengths are running along the flexible side of the card, and when you look at the card lengthways, you should be able to see the waviness of the corrugated card (see step 2).

DESIGNED BY
JAINA MINTON

METHOD

{01} Cut your cardboard

Enlarge the template on p. 140 and use it to draw out the cloud shape onto thick, 2-ply corrugated card. Cut it out on a cutting mat, using a craft knife and a metal ruler for the straight base edge.

To form the sides of your shelf, cut pieces of your 8cm (3⅛in) wide lengths of thin, single-layer corrugated card to match the circumference of each 'bump' of the cloud. The required lengths are marked on the template, but these may be 2–3mm (⅛in) out, depending on the thickness of your card, so measure each bump's circumference with a measuring tape to get accurate lengths.

{02} Assemble the cloud

Starting at the bottom left bump and working clockwise, tape each side on with sticky tape. To help the sides form around the curves, bend and flex the card (without creating a hard fold) a few times. Tape each bump to both the outside and the inside of the cloud to ensure it is well secured, making sure to leave no gaps in between (a).

Once all the curved sections are complete, cut a length of card to fit the straight section at the base of the cloud (no gaps) and securely tape in place. The cloud form or armature is complete and ready for the papier mâché (b).

{03} Apply the papier mâché

Apply at least two layers of papier mâché all over the card armature. Tear up pieces of newspaper or newsprint and paste on with a mix of PVA glue and water with a ratio of four parts glue to one part water. Use narrow, torn paper pieces (1cm/⅜in wide) to go around the curves, to ensure fewer creases and a better finish; you can use bigger torn pieces elsewhere. Make sure the papier mâché dries fully in between layers.

{04} Paint the cloud

Once the second layer of papier mâché is completely dry, paint the cloud interior with bright fluorescent paint, applying several layers if necessary to get a good coverage, and paint the exterior white.

{05} Cut the raindrops

Use the raindrop template (p. 140) to cut 32 raindrops from thin card. (Each raindrop will be made by sandwiching two raindrop pieces to make 16 raindrops.)

{02a}

{02b}

{03}

{06}

{07}

{09}

{06} Paint the raindrops

You need to make strands of raindrops in four colour groups of varying lengths: we used strands of four, five, three and four raindrops.

To create the painted ombre effect on each strand, paint the first pair of raindrops (remember two drops per finished raindrop) with your chosen paint colour. For the next pair, add a little white paint to your paint colour, and for the next pair, a little more white and so on, so that each shade is slightly more faded. Once all the raindrops are painted, leave them to dry.

{07} Assemble the raindrop strands

Cut a piece of thread approximately 60cm (24in) long. Working one colour group at a time, place one half of your first raindrop pair face down and spread some PVA glue onto the upturned side. Allowing for a free length of thread of around 10cm (4in) at the top, stick the thread onto the glued raindrop, then place the other half of the

pair on top to sandwich the thread in between. Allow for a gap of a few centimetres (1–2in) between raindrops. Cut off the excess thread after the last raindrop has been placed and leave to dry.

{08} Fix the raindrop strands to the cloud

Mark four dots at even intervals along the bottom of the cloud. Add a drop of superglue to each dot and carefully affix the threads at the top of the rainbow strands to the

marked dots. Leave to dry, then cut off any excess thread.

{09} Fix the picture hanging plate

Find the balance point at the top of the cloud and make a mark. Cut a hole with a craft knife that goes through one layer only of your 2-ply card – **do not go all the way through.** Position the hanging plate over the hole and attach it in place using lots of superglue. Once it is dry, your cloud shelf is ready to be hung.

Papercraft Story

I love scouting interior trends and finding ways of translating these into objects made from paper and card. My cloud shelf was inspired by the little house shelves so often seen in children's rooms. Anything made from paper has such a beautiful feel to it, and I will never grow bored of experimenting with it. *Jaina Minton*

Origami lampshade

If you thought origami was all about making small delicate models, think again. This lampshade will make a thrilling addition to your living room, and it's a great chance to practise some accordion folding. Success is all in the pre-creasing of the paper. The lampshade encloses perfectly around a ceiling light, as well as being suitable for large lampstands.

MATERIALS

Four sheets of medium-weight flat wrap paper, each measuring 50 x 70cm (20 x 27½in)

30cm (12in) diameter lampshade ring

Narrow double-sided tape approx. 5mm (¼in) wide

16 pieces of very narrow ribbon, each approx. 5cm (2in) long

60cm (24in) length of white self-adhesive hook-and-loop fastener

LED light bulb

SIZE

50cm (20in) wide x 24cm (9½in) high

FEATURED TECHNIQUES

- Origami (p. 118)

Papercraft Story

I have always been obsessed with making things, especially using paper. Even when I was at pre-school I remember endlessly making paper homes for my cuddly toys. When I was at school I was all about art, design and maths, a combination which never seemed to make sense to my teachers; but when I went to university to study graphic design, it quickly became evident that origami marries all three of my interests together!
Esther Thorpe

PRE-CREASE YOUR PAPER

{01} Take one sheet of flat wrap, with the patterned side face up, and fold in half horizontally.

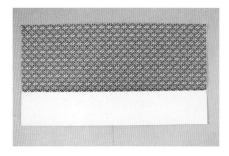

{02} Unfold. Now fold the bottom half of the paper up to the centre fold.

{03} Repeat to fold the top half of the paper to the centre. Unfold.

{04} Now fold the paper in half vertically.

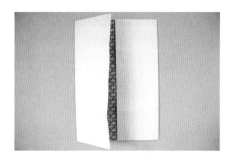

{05} Unfold, then fold both sides to the centre fold as shown and then unfold once again.

{06} Fold and unfold both the right-hand and left-hand edges to the pre-creases made in step 5.

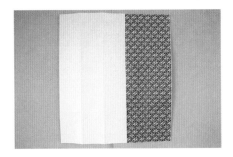

{07} Fold the left-hand edge to the second pre-crease from the right as in the photo, then unfold. Now fold the right-hand edge to the second pre-crease from the left, then unfold.

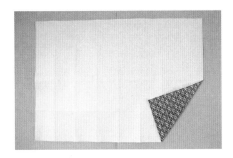

{08} The flat wrap should now resemble a grid of 32 equally distributed rectangles. Turn the paper over, so the patterned side is face down. Beginning in the bottom right-hand corner, fold diagonally from the horizontal centre fold through two rectangles, ensuring that the fold sits neatly in the rectangles. Unfold.

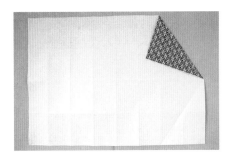

{09} Create a mirror image to the pre-crease in step 8, folding through the second rectangle down from the top right-hand corner through to the second rectangle along from the top right-hand corner. Unfold.

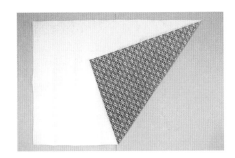

{10} Next pre-crease from the top right through four rectangles, again ensuring that the fold sits neatly through the rectangle, corner to corner. This fold should finish at the fourth rectangle from the bottom right. Unfold.

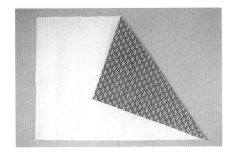

{11} Create a mirror image to the pre-crease in step 10, folding from the bottom right corner through four rectangles and finishing at the fourth rectangle from the top right.

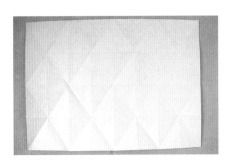

{12} You will begin to see a pattern emerging. Every diagonal fold through a rectangle is in the alternate direction to the rectangle it's next to. Continue with these alternate diagonal pre-creases until the whole grid is complete and every rectangle has one diagonal fold. Repeat steps 1–12 for each of the four flat wrap paper sheets.

METHOD

{01} Accordion fold each pre-creased sheet

Working on each pre-creased sheet in turn, pick up the paper with one of the shorter edges towards you and the pattern side facing up. Fold the pre-creases from one end of the paper to the other. This takes a little time to start, but once one end has begun to take shape, the rest of the folds become clearer. All the diagonal folds should be mountain folds and the vertical folds valley folds. Note: the horizontal pre-creases are not needed at this point.

Once you have completed the accordion folding of each of the four sheets, you have now made the four quarters of your lampshade.

{02} Prepare each unit

Working on each quarter unit in turn, adhere narrow strips of double-sided tape in between the smaller triangular shapes (a); these are now the top and bottom of the lampshade. Remove the backing from the strips and stick the smaller triangular sections together (b); there should be four sections to stick together at the top and the same at the bottom.

{03} Attach the quarter units to one other

Again, use strips of double-sided tape to attach each quarter unit to the next, positioning the tape along

{01}

{02a}

{02b}

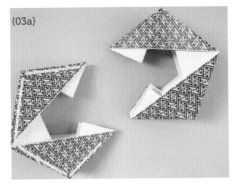

{03a}

{03b}

the top, bottom and side edges of the unit to be joined (a).

When joining the quarter units to each other, match edge to edge as accurately as possible (b).

{04} Fix the ribbons and hook-and-loop fastener in place

Once all four units are stuck together, use tape to fix two pieces of ribbon to every other inner section of the lampshade as centrally as possible. Measure and cut lengths of hook-and-loop fastener to the ends of the joined units, making sure to stick the

hook strips at one end and the loop strips at the other so that they can be joined together in step 5.

{05} Finish the lampshade

Tie the ribbons onto the lampshade ring, evenly distributing them around the frame so the paper can move together easily.

To use the lampshade, fix the lampshade ring to the cap and base of the light fitting and fit your LED light bulb. Close the lampshade round and seal with the hook-and-loop fastening.

{05}

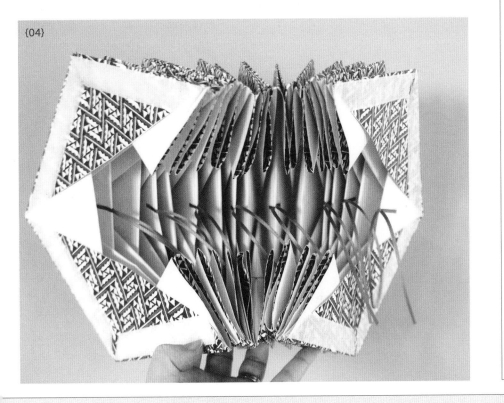
{04}

ESTHER THORPE
OF ORIGAMI-EST

ORIGAMI-EST originates from Esther Thorpe's passion for folding paper. Est is an avid origami fan and specialises in multi-modular origami creations. She enjoys celebrating the traditional Japanese art of paper folding while adding a contemporary edge. Est's origami is available to buy online and from a number of UK stockists. She also runs workshops in London and the seaside town of Deal. To find out more go to origamiest.co.uk

Sew pretty loop necklace

When it comes to making jewellery, paper is a versatile and inexpensive material, and it is also much tougher than you might think. This necklace combines retro-inspired shapes, stitched details and bold patterns to make an eye-catching piece that you're certain to enjoy creating and wearing.

DESIGNED BY KIRSTY NEALE

MATERIALS

Black mountboard

Paper: wood-grain and patterned

Needle and embroidery thread

12 jump rings

Five eyepins

Seven large round beads

50cm (20in) length of waxed thread or fine cord

PVA glue

Craft knife

Paper-piercing tool

Jewellery pliers

SIZE

Loops approx. 5 x 7.5cm (2 x 3in)
Finished length approx. 120cm (47in)

FEATURED TECHNIQUES

- Transferring templates (p. 104)
- Using a craft knife (p. 106)
- Stitching (p. 117)

BEFORE YOU BEGIN

You should be aware that cutting thick card like mountboard is likely to blunt the blade of your craft knife very quickly, and a blunt blade makes for messy, jagged edges. To keep your finished necklace looking as good as possible, change the blade as soon as you feel it start to drag, or if you notice any rough-cut edges.

Papercraft Story

I love working with mountboard. I'd describe it as a 'clean' cardboard – it has soft, smooth surfaces, with a colour of your choice on one side and a neat, white core. I like the fact that you can use it just as it comes with no need to paint or cover it up, unless you particularly want to, of course. It's good-looking, yet it is just as strong as other, more basic types of cardboard. The huge sheets go a long way, and I always keep a pile of scraps for smaller projects, too. Mountboard is definitely one of my go-to papercrafting supplies. *Kirsty Neale*

METHOD

{01} Cut the loops

To make the necklace as illustrated, you will need a total of six loops. Use the loop template (p. 138) to make a card template. Use the card template to draw out two loop shapes onto the black mountboard, and then cut out using a craft knife.

For the wood-grain and patterned paper loops, first stick a piece of your chosen paper to the mountboard and allow the glue to dry before cutting out your loop shapes; cut two from the wood-grain paper and two from the patterned paper.

{02} Prepare running-stitch loops

Use a pencil to draw an oval shape around the central hole on the reverse of each of the wood-grain loop shapes. Pierce holes at regular intervals following the pencil outline: each stitch is worked across two holes, so you'll need to pierce an even number of holes.

{03} Embroider running-stitch loops

Thread an embroidery needle with your chosen thread and knot the end. Taking your needle through from the back of the loop, sew a line of running stitches through the pierced holes. When you've finished, run the thread back through the last few stitches on the reverse of the loop to secure and snip off any excess. Apply a small amount of glue to the thread ends for extra security.

{04} Prepare cross-stitch loop

Draw out a series of crosses on the reverse of the loop, keeping them close to the edge of the central hole. Pierce holes in the corners of each marked 'X'.

{05} Embroider cross-stitch loop

Stitch a cross stitch through the pierced holes. It is possible to do this using the same length of embroidery thread by working the stitches in groups. Start by knotting the thread end and as you work each group, make sure to bring the thread down through the top right hole of the final cross (i.e. one of the holes slightly further away from the edge of the central hole), so that the thread easily crosses over to the top left hole of the first cross in the next group. Do make sure your thread still remains hidden on the back of the mountboard shape. Secure the thread ends as in step 3.

{03}

{05}

{06} Prepare starburst loops

Pierce a line of evenly spaced holes approximately 5mm (¼in) from the edge of the central hole.

{07} Embroider starburst loops

Thread the needle with your chosen thread and knot the end. Pull the needle through the first stitching hole, working from the reverse to the front. Take the needle back down through the centre of the loop, then return to pull it up through the second stitching hole and repeat, until you've stitched through all of the pierced holes.

After sewing through the final hole, take the needle back down through the centre of the loop, then pull it up through the previous stitching hole. The thread should form a small 'v' at the edge of the circle. Repeat, going back through each of the stitching holes in order, working around the circle in the opposite direction. When you've finished, secure the thread ends as in step 3.

Note

You may find it a little difficult to pull your needle through the pierced holes using just your fingers. If it feels too stiff, it may help to use a pair of jewellery pliers to get a better grip; hold the needle firmly without pulling too roughly.

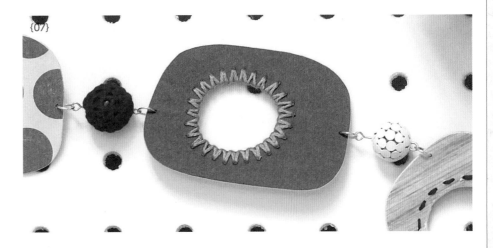

{07}

{08} Assemble the necklace

Pierce a hole in the centre of the short sides of each of the loops. Lay out the loops in your preferred order onto your work surface. Choose five beads to sit between the loops.

{09} Prepare beads for joining

Thread an eyepin through each bead. Use jewellery pliers to curve the straight end of each pin into a circle, so you have an 'eye' (tiny loop) at each side of the bead. (Depending on the size of the bead, you may need to snip off a piece of the eyepin before making the second eye.)

{10} Join loops and beads

Take your first loop and thread a jump ring through the hole at one side. Slide the eyepin at one end of a bead onto the same jump ring, then use pliers to close the ring. Thread another jump ring through the second loop and join the eye at the opposite end to the same ring. Close as before. You should now have a single bead, linking together two loops. Repeat to join all the loops together.

{11} Finish the necklace

Thread a jump ring through the final hole in the end loops and close. Knot one end of your waxed thread through one of the jump rings, leaving a tail of approximately 5mm (¼in). Slide a bead along the thread, so it sits snugly against the jump ring – the knot and tail should be hidden inside the bead. Slide on a second bead. Knot the opposite end of the thread around the final jump ring, leaving a short tail as before. Slide the second bead back along the thread to sit above the final jump ring, so hiding the knotted end.

Foxy nights paper cut

One-of-a-kind paper-cut designs make wonderful pictures, but if you take a scene and separate it into several pictorial elements, cut each from a different paper colour, then reconstruct the scene into a shadow box frame to create a 3D diorama, you will have something very special. In this diorama, two foxes meet for a midnight kiss while the city sleeps.

MATERIALS

Black box frame, 14 x 14 x 4.5cm (5½ x 5½ x 1¾in)

A3 sheets of thin card (or thick paper): one each in black, grey and mustard

Small piece of foam-core board

Double-sided tape

Mini foam mounting pads

Ballpoint pen and soft H pencil

Craft knife, cutting mat and metal ruler

SIZE

14 x 14 x 4.5cm (5½ x 5½ x 1¾in)

FEATURED TECHNIQUES

- Transferring templates (p. 104)
- Using a craft knife (p. 104)

Papercraft Story

For my picture of foxes in love, I wanted to use a black frame and three tones of paper to make a simple yet sophisticated paper-cut diorama. I love making 3D paper-cut scenes, often choosing to build my scene using just white paper for each of the layers, perhaps set against a colour backdrop. *Jaina Minton*

METHOD

{01} Trace the scenes onto the card
Use the templates on pp. 141–143 to transfer the three parts of the scene (including the outline of each square) onto coloured card as follows: kissing foxes on mustard, city skyline on grey, and night sky on black.

{02} Cut out the paper-cut designs
Referring to the photograph on p. 49 for the areas to be cut away on each of the designs, cut out each of the three scenes using a sharp craft knife and working onto a cutting mat. Also cut a piece of mustard card measuring 14 x 7cm (5½ x 2¾in): this is the final layer and, when it is positioned behind the night sky, it will illuminate the moon and the stars.

{03} Layer the city skyline and kissing foxes scenes
Cut two strips of foam-core board approximately 0.5 x 10cm

DESIGNED BY
JAINA MINTON

{01}

{02}

(¼ x 4in) and set one aside. From the remaining length, cut three smaller pieces and stick these onto the back of the kissing foxes layer with double-sided tape, positioning them as shown in the photo below, aligning them with the bottom edge and making sure that they cannot be seen from the front (a).

Attach another small piece of double-sided tape onto each length of the foam-core board strips to attach the kissing foxes layer to the city skyline, making sure the bottom and side edges line up exactly (b).

{04} Fit the layers into the box frame

Take the set-aside length of foam-core board and stick it to the bottom edge of the back of the city skyline, applying double-sided tape along one side of the foam-core board as well as along its base; remove backing and stick the front layers into the box frame.

Using the mini foam mounting pads, stick the mustard card rectangle to the top half of the night sky scene, so it shows behind the moon and the stars, ensuring you line up the edges exactly. Fit the layered night sky into the back of the frame, and assemble your box frame. Your picture is complete.

{03a}

{03b}

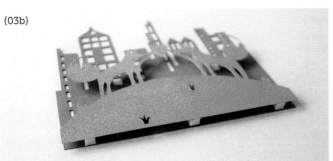

{04}

Pop-up teepee card

This fun pop-up is a great way to hone scoring and folding skills. With its teepee design, it would be great for a moving-house greeting or perhaps a send-off for a special trip. The decorations are inspired by Navajo patterns and they will provide plenty of practise for your fine cutting skills.

MATERIALS

A4 sheets of 135gsm paper: one each of pale grey and pale mint

A5 sheets of 135gsm paper: one each of dark grey, mint green, pale mint, pink, teal and yellow

One A4 sheet of teal 250gsm card

Craft knife, cutting mat and metal ruler

Bone folder and embossing tool

Tacky glue

SIZE

15 x 21cm (6 x 8¼in) closed, 30 x 21cm (12 x 8¼in) open

FEATURED TECHNIQUES

• Transferring templates (p. 104)
• Using a craft knife (p. 106)
• Scoring and folding (p. 108)

BEFORE YOU BEGIN

Using the templates on pp. 145–147, trace off and cut out from your A5 sheets of colour paper the templates required to decorate the front of the card and the teepee on the inside of the card, taking care not to get them mixed up.

Papercraft Story

I love the surprise of opening a pop-up card – I remember as a child being fascinated by them, and I am still just as fascinated now! Change your craft knife blade frequently, and my advice is to use an embossing tool to score with and a bone folder for crisp folds. Remember, papercraft should be fun, so be playful, and don't worry if it goes wrong, as you can just recycle it. *Sarah Matthews*

DESIGNED BY SARAH MATTHEWS

METHOD

{01} Cut out, score and fold the teepee templates

Enlarge and transfer the teepee template (p. 144) onto the A4 sheet of pale mint paper; transfer the teepee base template (p. 144) onto the A4 sheet of pale grey paper; cut both out.

Working on the teepee template, use an embossing tool and ruler to score along the dotted/dashed lines, then, using a bone folder, fold to create mountain or valley folds as marked on the template.

{02} Make and decorate base card

Take the A4 sheet of teal card and fold in half to give you an A5-sized base card. With the folded edge at the left-hand side, decorate the front of the card with your cut-out shapes to create the Navajo-inspired design. Start first with the placing of the large dark grey and mint green pieces in the centre, then layer up the pattern, following the photo on the opposite page for the order of application. Apply tacky glue to the back of each shape, spreading with a scrap of card to create a thin layer, before pressing down in place.

{03} Decorate the pop-up teepee

Working on the pale mint teepee piece, glue on the pattern pieces, building the design up in layers – the first layer of the decoration is shown being applied in the step photograph.

{04} Score the decorated pop-up teepee

Once all the pattern layers have been glued in place, and the pale grey base piece has been glued to line up with the bottom edge of the mint green piece, use your ruler and bone folder to score three lines over the decorated teepee in the same position as the underlying existing folds – this will define the shape of the teepee panels.

{05} Fold back the teepee flaps

Fold back the triangle on either side of the slit to create the entrance.

{06} Fold and glue decorated inner teepee panel

Carefully close the decorated panel so that the teepee is on the inside, encouraging the teepee to flatten outwards and ensuring that the folded teepee flaps lie flat. Rub all over the back of the folded inner

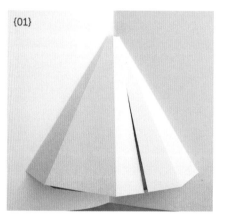
{01}

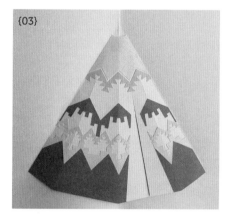
{03}

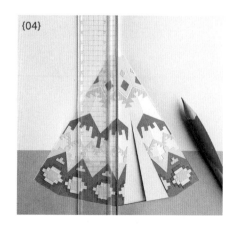
{04}

{05}

panel with the flat side of your bone folder, concentrating on the folds.

Open up the panel and turn over to work on the undecorated side. Apply a line of glue all the way around the outside of the teepee shape approximately 5mm (¼in) from the edge, and onto the central crease, above and below the teepee shape only (do not apply glue to the crease running through the middle of the teepee).

{06}

{07} Attach inner teepee panel to base card

Open up the base card (the decorated panel should be on the left-hand side of the reverse). Take the inner teepee panel and carefully position it, glue-side down, to align with the edges and the central fold of the base card, keeping it pressed down for a few seconds. Close and re-open the card, then leave it open to dry.

Instagram scrapbook picture

Scrapbooking is not just about life's big events – it's about capturing the everyday details too. Print your Instagram photos and put them on display in your home by making a scrapbook layout. Box frames are brilliant as they allow you to include lots of 3D textured elements, layering up pretty papers, shaped brads and other embellishments too.

MATERIALS

One sheet of 30 x 30cm (12 x 12in) scrapbooking paper

Selection of patterned papers

Selection of Instagram photos

Embellishments: decorative brads, wood veneer shapes, die-cut cardboard shape stickers, sequins, number stickers, silver doily

Embroidery thread and needle

Box frame, 30 x 30cm (12 x 12in)

Spray ink mists

Paper trimmer

Adhesives: PVA glue and foam mounting pads

SIZE

30 x 30cm (12 x 12in)

FEATURED TECHNIQUES

- Scrapbooking (p. 130)
- Presenting photographs (p. 131)
- Stitching (p. 117)

BEFORE YOU BEGIN

Decide on your subject: it could be a family wedding or a walk with friends. Print off a selection of your Instagram photos to give you plenty of choice.

If the photos you want to work with aren't gelling together, try printing them in black-and-white – this is a good trick to keep the look cohesive.

Daunted by the idea of composing your page? There are lots of great scrapbook templates online to start you off creating your own piece of art.

Papercraft Story

To see how fresh, modern and beautiful scrapbooking can be, visit sites like www.studiocalico.com or the work of some of my favourite paper artists – www.kellypurkey.typepad.com and www.lifelovepaper.com/blog. A great way to get into scrapbooking is through Becky Higgins' Project Life – http://beckyhiggins.com – it's an easy way to record your weeks and leave a lasting collection of beautiful art journaling. My memory is awful, so that's one of the reasons I scrapbook! *Lara Watson*

METHOD

{01} Gather your materials together

Select a good range of papers to layer up, as well as embellishments like decorative brads and die-cut stickers and shapes. Pick out a colour palette from your photos. Once you're happy with your selection of materials, trim your Instagram prints to size.

{02} Choose your background paper sheet

Decide which 30 x 30cm (12 x 12in) paper sheet you want to use as your background. It often helps to pick a block colour to build upon so that your accent papers and embellishments do the talking, and to ensure your final page doesn't look too cluttered.

To add a little interest to a block colour background, the overall effect can be helped by misting the paper with ink. Choose ready-to-spray inks from your selected colour palette. Place your sheet of paper in a cardboard box to protect your surroundings from splatters and spritz your ink. Your distance from nozzle to paper will obviously affect the look, so have a practise on a scrap piece of paper first. Try to stay at least 15cm (6in) away so that the ink dries quickly.

{03} Arrange your photos and embellishments

Now for the really fun bit. Start by arranging your selected photos and embellishments without sticking them down, thinking about composition as you go. It helps to 'anchor' the design on a strip of patterned paper, or mount your photos on paper to add a border (see pp. 131–132). Look for opportunities to add interest: having certain elements peeking out, such as the silver doily (top left) and the patterned paper placed at an angle (bottom right) works well. Collect a few embellishments together in clusters for impact, and think about the placement of your text or numbers as you go.

Once you are happy with the placement of photos and embellishments, take a picture on your phone or digital camera so that you can refer back to it as you build the page up in layers.

{01}

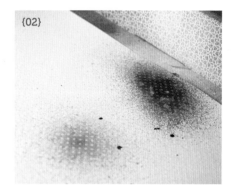
{02}

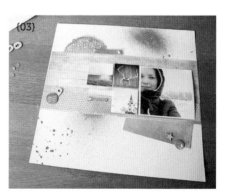
{03}

{04} Attach photos and embellishments to the page

Start fixing from the layer on top of the background paper and work up. Glue can warp paper, so use double-sided tape to fix the layers in place, and to help your photos stand out, adhere them with 3D foam mounting pads (a). Affix sequins and small embellishments with a tiny amount of PVA glue.

To add your brads, make a hole through the layers of paper with a needle or a pin first, placing a piece of foam underneath to support your paper and to stop it from bending and creasing. This technique also

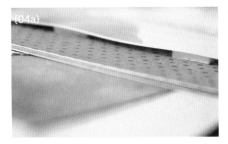

{04a}

works well when hand-stitching onto paper: create your holes first before threading the embroidery thread through (b), and fix the thread ends at the back of your paper sheet with a little tape.

{05} Frame the finished page

Once you're happy with your finished piece of work, pop it in your box frame so that your embellishments don't get squished. Now all that is left to do is to hang it on the wall or to prop it on a shelf for a lasting keepsake.

LARA WATSON

Lara is Editor of *Mollie Makes* magazine and a fan of lots of crafts. Her first crafty love, however, is paper. Lara is a regular contributor to *Papercraft inspirations* magazine, and always has a crate of handmade cards available for emergencies. She's also a writer, event speaker and occasional stylist. For more, see @laramcspara

{04b}

Capital letter pennant

Make your mark with this pennant-style wall hanging and its eye-catching 3D monogram, all made from paper and card. Choose and cut your letter form from card, then wrap it with newspaper to give it shape, and decorate with stripy tissue paper to finish. Hang it on the wall above your bed.

MATERIALS

One A3 sheet of thick 2-ply (double-layer) corrugated card

A3 sheets of coloured card: one each of grey and mauve

Patterned tissue paper

Foam-core board letter (see Before You Begin)

Tape: masking, sticky and double-sided

Adhesives: PVA and superglue

Acrylic paint and paintbrush

1m (1yd) length of string

Craft knife, cutting mat and metal ruler

Soft H pencil and ballpoint pen

Scissors

SIZE

26 x 59cm (10⅛ x 23⅛in)

FEATURED TECHNIQUES

- Transferring templates (p. 104)
- Using a craft knife (p. 106)

BEFORE YOU BEGIN

Prepare your foam-core board letter in advance. Choose the letter style you prefer from royalty-free fonts (we have used a very elegant, curling font) and print it out as large as you can onto A4 paper. Place the print-out face down onto a light box or a window, and make a tracing of the reverse of the letter with a soft H pencil. Turn your tracing over and place it onto a piece of A4 foam-core board and go over it using a ballpoint pen. The letter will now appear on the foam-core board the right way around; carefully cut it out using a craft knife.

METHOD

{01} Cut and paint card pennant

Enlarge the pennant template on p. 140 and use to cut out a pennant from thick corrugated card. To neaten the edges, tape masking tape along each cut edge. Paint over the taped edge with grey acrylic paint (or any other neutral colour of your choice) and leave to dry.

{02} Complete decoration

Now to decorate the pennant with a paper chevron design. First, use the complete template to cut a pennant from mauve-coloured card and attach it to the corrugated card pennant using double-sided tape. Then cut the chevron from the bottom of the pennant template and use to cut two chevrons from the grey-coloured card. Attach one of the chevron arrows to align with the bottom edge of the pennant. Measure 20cm (8in) from the bottom point of the pennant, lining up through the centre, and make a mark. Align the point of the second chevron arrow with the mark you have just made and tape it in place; trim off the excess paper at the top of the pennant.

{03} Attach the hanging string

Take your length of string, tie it in a loop, and tape it down along the top edge on the back of the pennant. Add some dabs of superglue where the string angles up at each corner and leave to dry.

{01}

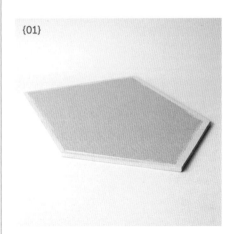

{02}

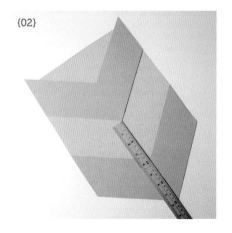

{03}

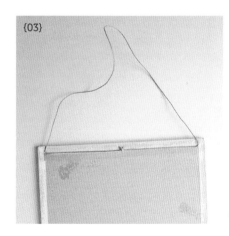

Papercraft Story

Paper is always my preferred choice of medium. I'm drawn to its tactile loveliness. Sculpting with newspaper is a very physical way of working and quite tough on the hands, but it's cheap, relatively mess-free, and can be done anywhere. I started using this technique for simple forms specifically for children, but discovered that, with practise, it's possible to make detailed and complex sculptures too. *Jaina Minton*

DESIGNED BY JAINA MINTON

{04} Paper sculpt the letter

Now to turn your foam-core board letter into a 3D form. Tear out a page from a newspaper and scrunch it up into a ball. Un-scrunch and scrunch it up again to make the paper really soft and malleable. Tear off small pieces from the conditioned paper and begin to roll it up into shapes to lay on top of the letter to begin to form a more rounded shape (a). The shapes you require will depend on your letter style, but use simple shapes such as balls or sausage shapes. Stick the paper shapes on with sticky tape, and build up the shape using small pieces as you go (b). Stick tape over the sculpted newspaper in small pieces and press hard to get a smooth finish.

{05} Decorate the sculpted letter

Paint the finished letter with white acrylic paint, then decorate it with a patterned paper of your choosing. Tissue paper works best as it applies to the curves easier. Paste on PVA glue and small strips of the paper to cover the whole letter. Leave to dry completely, then stick the decorated letter onto the centre of your banner using superglue.

{04a}

{04b}

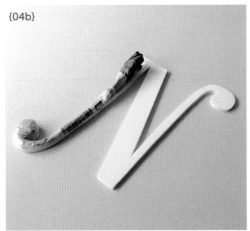

{05}

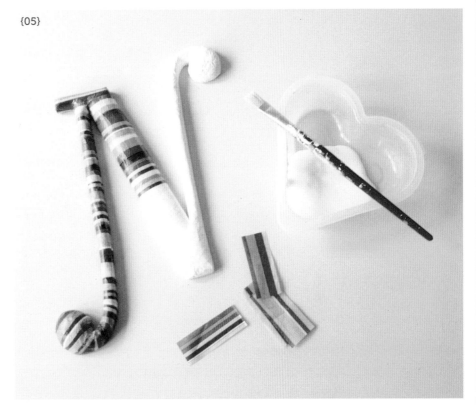

Mini party piñata

Traditionally made from papier mâché, filled with sweet treats and covered with brightly coloured decorations, a piñata is hung high and hit with a stick until it splits sending its goodies falling to the ground. Treat your guests to these cute watermelon slices — but to release the stash from these mini piñatas, all they need to do is pull the string!

MATERIALS

One A4 sheet of white card

Crêpe paper rolls: lime green and pink

Small pieces of metallic pink and blue card (or paper)

Narrow ribbon

Small sweets and treats

Adhesives: glue stick and masking tape

Scissors

SIZE

12cm (4¾in) along widest edge

FEATURED TECHNIQUES

- Transferring templates (p. 104)
- Scoring and folding (p. 108)
- Paper manipulation: Fringing (p. 110)

BEFORE YOU BEGIN

Prepare your crêpe paper: cut strips of pink paper 12 x 3cm (4¾ x 1⅛in) and strips of lime green paper 18 x 3cm (7 x 1⅛in); fringe one side of the paper strips using a pair of scissors. Note, if you fold the crêpe paper first you can cut and fringe several strips at once.

Trace off the watermelon templates (A and B) from pp. 152–153 onto card and cut out to give you card templates A and B. Score the folds marked with dashed lines.

ELLEN DEAKIN
OF HAPPYTHOUGHT

Ellen and Harry met at the Glasgow School of Art where they studied graphic design and product design respectively. After a decade of working in the design and music industry they launched Happythought, an online store and blog full of craft ideas and fun printable paper crafts. They are currently based in Chile with their two young children, Harvey and Missy. For more, see www.happythought.co.uk

Papercraft Story

Our move to Chile, and the colourful birthday parties we have attended here, have been the inspiration behind this project. Without fail, every children's party ends with a piñata, which come in all shapes and sizes; in the streets of our local town, you can find many vendors selling homemade piñatas and doing a roaring trade. **Ellen Deakin**

METHOD

{01} Decorate card template A

Take the middle section of your watermelon (template A) and cover one side of the card with glue. Starting from the bottom, apply strips of pink fringed crêpe paper, overlapping each strip as shown, and continue until you reach the middle of the card (a).

Now turn the card through 180 degrees and repeat to decorate the other half of the card in the same way. Turn the decorated card over and trim off the excess fringing (b).

{02} Prepare card template B

Make a hole as indicated on the long tabbed strip on card template B, then cover with lime green fringing, taking care not to block the hole; trim off excess paper.

Turn template B over and attach a loop of the narrow ribbon (the hanging loop) to the middle of the oval with masking tape, as shown in the photo. Take a smaller length of ribbon and thread it through the hole in the tabbed strip; secure it on the reverse with a knot and attach a piece of masking tape over the knot to secure – this is the pull ribbon to release the goodies.

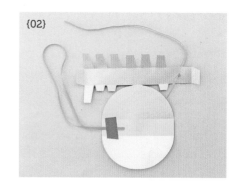

{02}

{03} Assemble the watermelon slice

Turn template B back to the right side and glue template A on top, aligning it to the marked oval. Apply glue to all of the tabs and assemble, leaving tab marked C open for now.

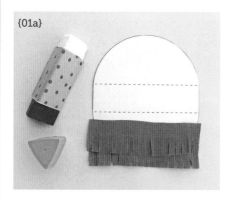

{01a}

{01b}

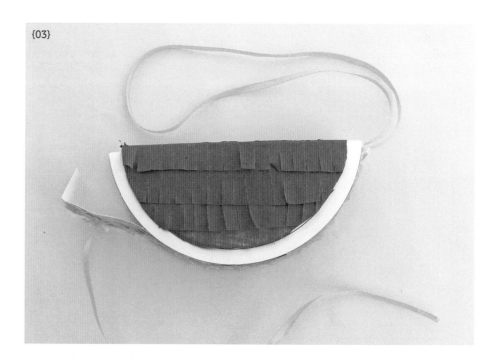

{03}

{04} Finish the watermelon slice

Carefully cut the pull tab template (p.152) from metallic pink card. Fold it in half and glue it onto the end of the ribbon. Cut out 10 seeds from metallic blue card and glue them in place, five on either side.

Take the remaining fringed strips of crêpe paper and cut the ends off to make tiny colourful squares. This is your confetti. If you have it, add some colourful glitter, too. Fill the piñata with the confetti and add some small sweets, then seal by lightly gluing tab C in place.

{04}

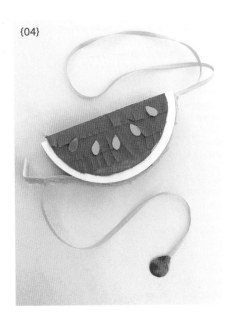

To release the goodies inside, just pull the ribbon!

Folded flowerball

Guaranteed to impress, the Kusudama flowerball is the perfect introduction to multi-modular origami. Each petal unit is made from a square of paper, and with 60 petals required for the 12 flowers that make up the flowerball, you'll be a very confident folder by the time you complete it.

MATERIALS

60 squares of 90–120gsm origami paper 15 x 15cm (6 x 6in)

Extra-strong, quick-drying glue

40cm (16in) length of ribbon

SIZE

22cm (8⅝in) diameter

FEATURED TECHNIQUES

• Origami (p. 118)

BEFORE YOU BEGIN

Practise folding the petal units on spare sheets of origami paper, following Fold the Petal Units on p. 70. Once you have achieved perfectly sculpted petals, you can move on to fold the petals from your preferred choice of origami paper.

DESIGNED BY ESTHER THORPE

Papercraft Story

Throughout my degree and since, I have enjoyed stretching myself with more and more complex models, and I still find so much satisfaction transforming 2D square sheets into something beautiful to decorate my home.
Esther Thorpe

FOLD THE PETAL UNITS

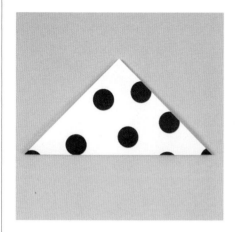

{01} Take a sheet of paper, un-patterned side face up, and fold it in half diagonally.

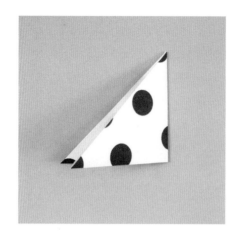

{02} Fold the paper in half diagonally again as shown, then unfold.

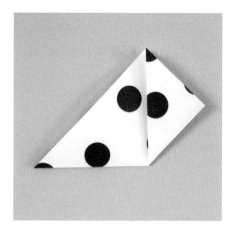

{03} Fold the bottom right-hand corner to the top.

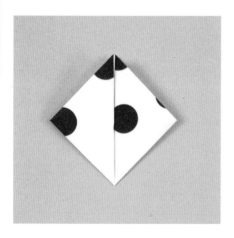

{04} Fold the bottom left-hand corner to the top. You now have a diamond shape.

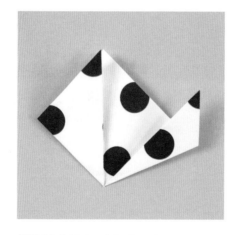

{05} Unfold the right-hand side, then fold the bottom right-hand edge to the diagonal pre-crease created in step 3.

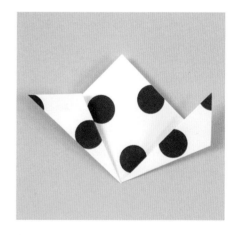

{06} Fold the left-hand side back to the diagonal edge created in step 4.

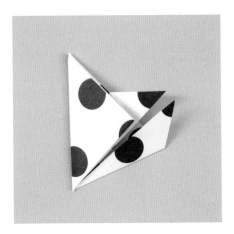

{07} Fold the unit in half (folding left-hand side to right-hand side) along the centre pre-crease made in step 2.

{08} Fold the right-hand triangle over to tuck it behind the top layer of the model.

{09} Your model should now look like this.

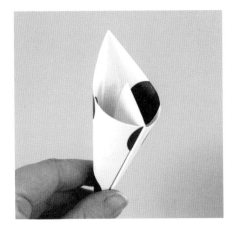

{10} Begin to gently squeeze your model back and front between the fingers of one hand to slightly flex and begin to shape the sides to the petal shape.

{11} To fix the petal shape, fold over the small triangles (folding them to the left), to lock the layers in place. You have created one petal.

{12} Use your fingers to sculpt the petal into a shape you're happy with. Make a total of 60 petal units.

METHOD

{01} Join five petals to make one flower

Take one petal, and using your fast-drying, extra-strong glue, join another petal to it (a). Then join another petal (b), each time working as close to the folded edges as possible. Continue until a total of five petal units have been joined to make one flower (c). Repeat to make a total of 12 flowers.

{02} Join six flowers together to make a flowerball half

Working one at a time, attach the outer edges together using fast-drying, extra-strong glue (a). When three flowers have been joined, take your ribbon and glue it to two of the adjoining flowers, so the ends are glued to a depth of at least 4cm (1½in) (b). Continue to glue the flowers together until you have joined all six to form a semi-spherical flowerball.

Note

You could try folding your petal units with paper that has a different pattern on each side to highlight the shape of the individual flowers. Or try a metallic flecked paper to make a version for Christmas.

{01a}

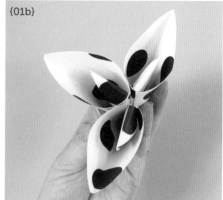
{01b}

{01c}

{02a}

{02b}

{03} Make a second flowerball half

Join the remaining six flowers to form a second semi-spherical flowerball, but this one does not need to have a hanging loop fixed in place.

{04} Complete the flowerball

Glue the two flowerball halves together using fast-drying, extra-strong glue and ensuring the flower edges are lined up to one another. Hang your completed flowerball.

{03}

Forest friends shelf ornaments

This colourful trio are fun to make and a good way to brighten up a dull corner. Make them bold and bright to appeal to your inner child, or, if you prefer, choose more natural tones to appeal to the Mother Earth within you. Either way, discover just how easy a little DIY stamping can be.

MATERIALS

Four A4 sheets of a heavyweight white paper

A4 sheets of card stock: one each of bright orange, bright red and bright pink

Recycled card packaging and double-sided tape for making stamps

White poster paint

Felt-tip pens

Scissors

Glue stick

Fine paintbrush

Pencil with eraser on its end

SIZE

Squirrel: 12.5cm (4⅞in)
Rabbit: 15.5cm (6in)
Owl: 11.5cm (4½in)

FEATURED TECHNIQUES

- Transferring templates (p. 104)
- Using a craft knife (p. 106)
- Scoring and folding (p. 108)
- Stamping: Making your own stamps (p. 115)

Papercraft Story

At Happythought we love the endless possibilities in folding and cutting a simple sheet of paper. Our emphasis is on producing projects for all the family that not only look lovely but are easy to make with just scissors, card and a glue stick – minimum fuss for maximum fun! But I couldn't resist adding a little bit of decoration to this trio with some geometric-shaped stamps made from recycled card. *Ellen Deakin*

METHOD

{01} Prepare the animal templates
Copy the animal templates (pp. 149–151) onto your heavyweight white paper sheets and cut them out. Keep all the parts together that make up each animal.

{02} Use templates to cut animal pieces from coloured card
Working one animal at a time, draw around the templates onto your chosen coloured card stock to transfer all the parts you need to make the animal. Carefully cut out your animal pieces.

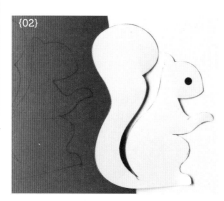

{03} Prepare your DIY stamps
To make the stamps for decorating the squirrel and the rabbit, cut out a triangle and an oblong from thick card packaging and stick each onto a larger piece of cardboard using double-sided tape. For the circular stamp, simply use the rubber on the end of a pencil.

It is a good idea to practise your stamping onto a scrap of paper before moving on to decorate your card animals. For a neater finish, use a fine brush to apply the paint onto your stamp.

{04} Decorate the rabbit
Stamp with the oblong stamp over the front of the rabbit's body. Use a paintbrush to add detailing to the inner ears, the tips of the feet, the bobtail and the eye. Also, paint the paws on the end of the arms. When dry, add felt-tip pen detail to eye.

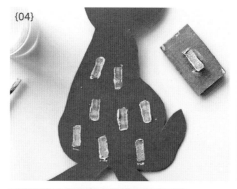

{05} Decorate the squirrel
Stamp with the triangle stamp to add a decorative pattern to the squirrel's front piece. You can either do this randomly (as shown in the step photo) or along the spine only, as shown on the finished squirrel on p. 75. Use a paintbrush to add the eyes. When dry, add felt-tip pen detail to eye.

{06} Decorate the owl
Stamp with the eraser end of the pencil to make rows of circles all the way down the front of the owl's

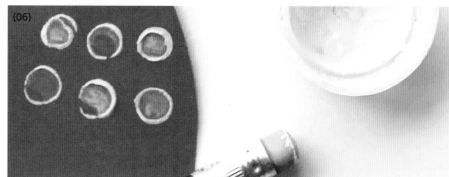

body. Use a paintbrush to paint eye circles on one side, and, when dry, add felt-tip pen detail. Shade in the triangle part of the beak on one side.

{07} Construct the rabbit

Fold the rabbit's legs up onto the body along the dotted line (see template), then fold back so that they sit at a right-angle to the body.

Fold the arms along the dotted lines (see template) to make the tabs to attach them to the rabbit's chest with glue, but first roll (paw sides facing up) over a pencil to curl forwards. Fix the whiskers in place.

{08} Construct the squirrel

Stick the squirrel templates together along the spine, from the top of the head to the base of the body; do not glue to the right of the dotted line (see template). Splay the legs out so that the squirrel stands up. Fix the acorn in place between its paws.

{09} Construct the owl

Snip the ear tufts at either side of the head and roll the card at the top forwards over a pencil to shape.

Snip all the way around the outside of the eye circles and stick onto the owl's head. Fold the beak along the dotted line to make a tab to fix it between the eyes.

Score and fold the wings along the dotted lines. Take the larger wing and glue the inside back. Slip the wing over the right-hand side of the body and press in place – the wing should be left unstuck at the front of the owl. Fix the smaller wing as before, placing it on top of the larger wing to align at the top edges.

Fold the stand along the dotted line, glue the smaller portion and attach it to the base of the owl's body so that the unstuck piece angles out to support the owl.

{07}

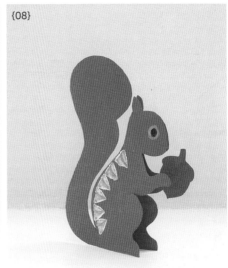

{08}

DESIGNED BY
ELLEN DEAKIN

{09}

Quilling shadow box

This simple-but-bold piece of abstract wall art takes its inspiration from traditional quilling techniques, yet you don't need a quilling tool to make it – just a humble toothpick will do. Nestling together inside a handmade shadow box frame, coiled paper circles of varying sizes and depths are made in a rainbow of colours.

MATERIALS

One sheet of white mountboard, 50 x 30cm (20 x 12in)

Sheets of coloured paper with a colour core

White acrylic paint and small paintbrush

Adhesives: PVA glue and glue stick

Craft knife, cutting mat and metal ruler

Pencil and toothpick

DESIGNED BY KIRSTY NEALE

SIZE

17.5 x 17.5 x 2cm (6⅞ x 6⅞ x ¾in)

FEATURED TECHNIQUES

- Transferring templates (p. 104)
- Scoring and folding (p. 108)
- Quilling (p. 122)

BEFORE YOU BEGIN

Scoring the mountboard to make the box frame base is a little tricky – try practising on a few pieces of scrap card to get the hang of it first. You need to score firmly enough that the card will fold easily, but not so hard that you slice right through it.

Short of time? You can omit making the frame altogether and use a store-bought shadow box frame instead.

It is important that the colour paper used for the quilling strips are dyed rather than colour-printed, as the core will be visible when the paper is coiled. Patterned papers generally have a white core – the pattern is printed onto a white base and only coats the surface – but basic art paper should be a good choice.

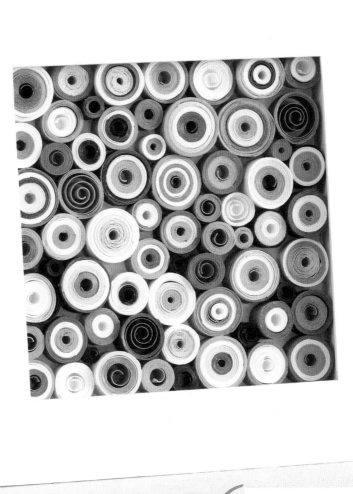

METHOD

{01} Make the box frame patterns and use to cut the mountboard
Take a large sheet of tracing paper and make a pattern for both the front frame and box frame base using the measurements on the templates on pp. 154–155 as your guide.

Use the front frame pattern to transfer the cutting lines to the back of the mountboard sheet and cut out using a craft knife. Set the front frame piece aside.

Use the box frame base pattern to transfer the scoring (dashed) and cutting lines (solid black) onto the right side of the mountboard and the middle square (light grey outline) onto the back of the mountboard only. Working on the right side of the mountboard sheet, use a craft knife to cut out around the solid line only.

{02} Assemble the box frame base
Working on the front of the mountboard, use a craft knife to gently score along the dashed lines: remember, you need to score firmly enough that the card will fold easily, but not so hard that you slice right through it. Fold along each of the scored lines towards the wrong side of the mountboard.

With the wrong side of the mountboard face up, add glue to one cut edge of the card A and press it down directly onto line A of the

marked square to create one side of the box frame base. Hold in place for a few minutes until the glue begins to dry (a).

Repeat for B, C and D to make the other three sides of the frame, adding extra glue to the corners where each of the pieces meet (b).

Squeeze a bead of glue along each of the scored, folded edges to create a smoother finish. Allow the glue to dry, then brush a coat of white acrylic paint all over the outside edges and interior of the box frame base; set aside to dry.

{03} Prepare the paper strips
Cut your coloured papers into strips. For the picture as illustrated, 1cm (⅜in) and 1.3cm (1½in) wide strips were used, but you can vary the widths as you wish. The length of the strips will be dependent on the size of your paper, but ideally they should be at least 30cm (12in) long.

{04} Roll the coils
Take a paper strip and start to coil it around the toothpick (a). Try to keep it as tight as you can as you continue to roll it (b). Once you have

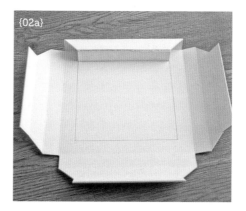
{02a}

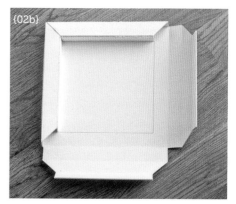
{02b}

Note
Once you have scored and folded-over the mountboard to make the box frame base, these sections will be a slightly different colour. A coat of acrylic paint will help to neaten them off, and this is especially important if you are using a coloured mountboard as these may be visible on the frame from some angles. There is no need to paint the reverse of the box frame base as this will not be seen at all once hung.

made the coil as big as you want it to be, glue down the end to fix the shape. Continue to make as many coils as you need to fill your frame (it took around 80 to make the picture illustrated).

Make tight coils in the main, but for variety make a few looser (open) circles. To create multi-coloured pieces, attach the end of a contrast strip to the outside of a coil, and carry on wrapping it around the outside. Vary the length of strips to create wider or narrower bands of colour. It is also worth making a few smaller coils from shorter strips as these will be useful for filling small gaps in your finished picture.

{05} Assemble the picture

Once you've quilled a good selection of coils in your chosen colours you can begin arranging them inside the box frame base. Place the pieces one at a time, starting in a corner and gradually working your way outwards. Keep a good balance of colours and vary coil sizes.

When you are happy with the design, you can start sticking the pieces into place. Carefully lift out each coil, working on one at a time. Spread a very thin layer of adhesive over the base of the coil using a toothpick, then press it back into position, before lifting out the next coil and repeating. Work methodically, sticking down one piece at a time.

{06} Finish off

Take the set-aside front frame and glue to the front edges of the box frame base. It should slightly overhang the inner and outer edges.

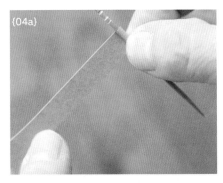

{04a}

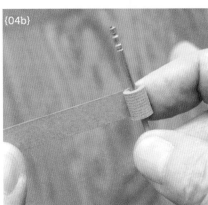

{04b}

Teeny-weeny pull-out house

This miniature paper house makes a great alternative to a standard greeting card. Just open the roof to reveal pull-out pages that carry your message. Particularly fitting for a new house gift, you can easily ring the changes to make a pull-out house suitable for any card-giving occasion.

MATERIALS

One A4 sheet of thick paper or thin card in a colour of your choosing

Decorative embellishments: buttons, lace, sewing thread, ribbon and miniature key charm

Small piece of white paper

PVA glue and glue spreader

Craft knife, cutting mat and metal ruler

Scissors

Bone folder

Pen and pencil

SIZE

4cm (1½in) wide x 7cm (2¾in) high

FEATURED TECHNIQUES

• Transferring templates (p. 104)
• Using a craft knife (p. 106)
• Scoring and folding (p. 108)

Papercraft Story

In my work I hand-make everything from start to finish using skills in traditional book-binding, woodwork, textiles and papercraft. For the mini house pull-out I took my inspiration from the 'pull-out' book works that I developed when I became interested in playing around with the idea of what a book could be.
Alix Swan

METHOD

{01} Prepare your house template

Transfer the house template (p. 148) to your thick paper sheet. Score along the marked (dotted) score lines using a metal ruler and the back of a craft knife, being careful not to cut through the paper. Cut out the template along the solid lines, not forgetting the chimney and the slit for closing the roof.

{02} Cut and score pull-out pages

Cut a strip of your paper measuring 21 x 4cm (8¼ x 1½in). Measure 1cm (⅜in) from one short end at top and bottom and make a pencil mark (this is the attachment tab). Now measure and make a pencil mark every 4cm (1½in) at top and bottom along the full length of the strip. Use a pencil to lightly draw lines between the corresponding marks. Use a ruler to join top and bottom marks and score along the lines. Concertina fold (see p. 109).

{03} Decorate the house

Before assembling the house, add a little decoration using a fine pen. For example, draw a front door with the recipient's door number, add flowers and grasses to give a country cottage vibe, and roughly sketch out tiles on the roof and chimney.

{04} Decorate the pull-out pages

Leaving the first narrow strip undecorated (this is the tab for attaching the pages to the house in step 5), continue to draw flowers and grasses along the bottom edge of the pull-out pages. Decorate your pages as you please: for our house, on pages 1 and 5 window apertures were cut to contain 'floating' hearts (cut from two pieces of ribbon with sewing thread sandwiched in between); on page 2, a mini envelope was made (see template p. 148) to contain a secret message; on page 3, a mini key charm was glued on; and on page 4, a door was cut to repeat the front door motif.

{05} Construct and finish the house

Using a glue spreader, apply glue carefully to each tab and stick together to make the house (a).

To create the windows, add thread to buttons before gluing in place. Add a narrow lace trim along the top of the house by carefully placing a small amount of glue along the top of the paper.

Apply glue carefully to the attachment tab on pull-out pages and fix to the inside of the house (b).

ALIX SWAN

Alix Swan is a paper and mixed media artist who collects old books of vintage stories, rhymes and fairy tales. She makes traditional books as well as 3D illustrated mixed-media pieces – sometimes including vintage music boxes – to re-tell well-loved stories. Her treasure trove of 'little bits and pieces' inspires her work. For more, see www.facebook.com/alixswan. littlebitsofprintythings or @alixprintybits

{05a}

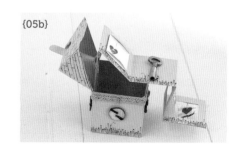

{05b}

Paper and wire bird

This little blue tit is made from a wire base covered in little scraps of coloured paper torn from magazines. You can make any bird you choose. Just find a picture of the bird you want to make to give you a guide to its markings, and select your coloured papers to match.

MATERIALS

White tissue paper

Scraps of paper in yellow, bright blue, darker blue, pale green, black and white, torn from magazines

Thin florist's wire

PVA glue and paintbrush

Wire cutters and pair of small pliers

Black pen

SIZE

5cm (2in) high and 10cm (4in) from beak to tail

FEATURED TECHNIQUES

• Papier mâché: Making armatures (p. 129)

BEFORE YOU BEGIN

For this project, wire is used to build up a shape over which the papier mâché is worked. Thin florist's wire is used as this is very easy to manipulate. Use wire cutters to cut the wire and a pair of small pliers to pinch and fashion the wire into shape. Pointed-nose pliers used for jewellery-making are ideal.

Prepare your papier mâché papers in advance: tear up the white tissue paper into pieces no larger than 1cm (³/₈in) wide, and your yellow, bright blue, darker blue and pale green magazine scraps into very small pieces measuring approximately 5mm (¼in) square, keeping each pile separate. Tear the black scraps into very thin strips.

DESIGNED BY
CLARE YOUNGS

Papercraft Story

I try to use recycled paper when crafting as much as possible. I salvage bits of card to use as a base for projects and I use old labels, stamps and bits of packaging in my designs. I am always on the lookout for different types of paper, scouring car boot sales and secondhand shops for out-of-date maps and musical scores.

Clare Youngs

METHOD

{01} Make the bird's body

Wind up some wire to make a ball about the size of an egg. Cut off the end and tuck it into the middle of the ball. Pinch the ball into more of a body and head shape and pull out a bit of the folded wire to make the beak at the head end.

{02} Make the bird's tail

Thread a length of wire through the body section at the back of the bird and bend it around to make a tail shape approximately 2.5cm (1in) long (a). Wind the wire back and forth across the tail (b). Cut the wire and hide any spare wire within the body of the bird.

{03} Make the bird's legs and feet

Cut a piece of wire 50cm (20in) long. Fold the wire back by approximately 16cm (6¼in) at one end. Working at the folded end of the wire, pinch about 1cm (⅜in) and twist to make a toe. Form the wire alongside the toe into a loop 1cm (⅜in) long and twist to make a second toe (a). Repeat to make the third toe, then twist the double section of wire to join the wires together (b).

Thread the wire through the underside of the bird's body so that there is a 1cm (⅜in) gap between the legs (c). Make a second leg to match the first leg, then cut off any excess wire.

{04} Papier mâché the wire bird

Use watered-down PVA glue to stick overlapping pieces of white tissue paper to the bird's body and tail, leaving the legs and feet uncovered. Apply two layers.

Now add the coloured paper markings, working in the following order: yellow on the bird's breast, stopping at the neck; darker blue all along each side of the bird and all over the tail, mixing in a few pieces of the brighter blue along the side of the bird and the wing area; pale green all along the bird's back tapering down to a point towards the tail; black strips to make the ring around the neck and the three stripes radiating out from the beak on the head.

Take a scrap of white and draw on two eyes using the black pen, leaving the centre of each eye as a white dot. Cut out the eyes and fix in position (see photo) with a dot of glue. To finish, stick some of the bright blue paper scraps in a circle on the top of the head.

{02a}

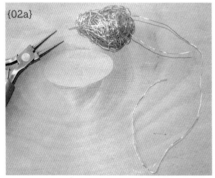

{02b}

{03a}

{03b}

{03b}

{04}

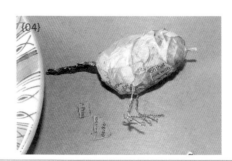

Three little cacti pots

These three cacti plants will bring an everlasting touch of nature to your desk. Not only do they look beautiful but they are useful too. Lift the lids to reveal little pots for paper clips, drawing pins and loose change. Their bold, geometric patterns and paper-sculpted shapes will put your cutting, scoring, folding and slotting skills to the test.

MATERIALS

A4 sheets of 135gsm paper: one each of pale green, dark green, pale grey, medium grey and dark grey

A5 sheets of 135gsm paper: one each of yellow, pink, orange, tan and brown

Craft knife, cutting mat and metal ruler

Bone folder and embossing tool

Tacky glue

Scissors

White pen, pencil and rubber

SIZE

Tall, thin and slotted cacti:
Approx. 16cm (6¼in) high

Spiky spherical cactus:
Approx. 10.5cm (4⅛in) high

Succulent:
Approx. 8cm (3⅛in) high

FEATURED TECHNIQUES

- Transferring templates (p. 104)
- Scoring and folding (p. 108)
- Paper manipulation: Tabbing (p. 110)

Papercraft Story

I love cacti and succulents, partly because I can actually keep them alive, but mostly for their form, repetition and the beauty of their natural geometric shapes. I created this trio as I wanted to design something practical but playful, to add some colour to my workspace. I enjoyed using a variety of paper manipulation methods to create the 3D forms of the differently shaped cacti.
Sarah Matthews

METHOD

{01} Cut your coloured paper

Cut out pieces from your coloured papers following the cutting instructions on the templates on pp. 156–158. There are a lot of pieces to be cut, so do try to keep them together in an organised fashion to make locating them as you need them easier (a).

Use an embossing tool and ruler to score along the dotted lines and a bone folder to crease along your scored lines, creating either a mountain or valley fold as marked on the templates.

{02} Decorate the dark green paper pieces

Using a white pen, draw dots all over both sides of the dark green pieces for the slotted cactus pieces. Then draw dashes in random directions down the front edges of the elliptical dark green pieces of the spiky spherical cactus pieces, as well as in the centre of the spiky circles.

DESIGNED BY
SARAH MATTHEWS

{01}

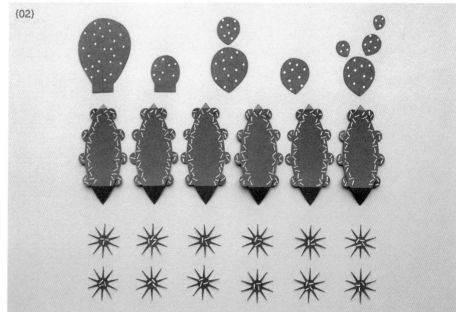

{02}

{03} Make three pot bases

Take one of the large pot pieces (template A) and fold the tabs upwards (a). Taking a small paper circle in the same colour, apply glue approximately 5mm (¼in) from the edge.

Now fix the large pot piece on top of the glued circle, beginning to curve it so that the tabs overlap the circle to point inwards and line up with the edge of the circle. Glue the overlapping edges of the pot piece together (b). Apply a thin layer of glue over the back of the matching small circle piece and press it inside the base of the pot.

{04} Make three pot lids

Take one of the tabbed narrow curved strips (template B) and fold the tabs upward. Taking a large paper circle in the same colour, apply glue approx 5mm (¼in) from the edge. Begin to curve the strip around so that its edges overlap and the tabs are facing up and pointing inwards. Hold the circle, glue side up, beneath the curved strip and push it up to the tabs from below. Glue the overlapping edges of the strip together (a).

Apply a thin layer of glue all the way around the outside edge of the lid, then take the un-tabbed curved strip of the same colour (template C) and press it around the edge so that the bottom edges line up and the top of the strip stands proud from the rest of the lid (b).

{05} Make the succulent

To decorate the pot plant, spread a thin layer of glue over the back of the yellow triangle strip and glue it around the bottom edge of the dark grey pot. Glue a large tan circle on top of the pot lid to cover the tabs.

Take the three pale green succulent pieces and individually fold each petal upwards. Apply a thin layer of glue to the back centre of the smallest piece and glue it on top of the medium-sized piece, so that it is central and the small petals lie in between the medium petals. Then glue this joined piece onto the largest piece in the same way, and then glue the whole 'flower' onto the lid.

{03a}

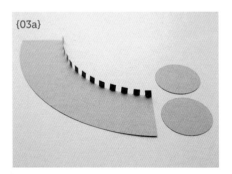

{04a}

{03b}

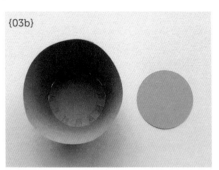

{04b}

{05}

{06} Make the spiky spherical cactus

To decorate the pot plant, spread a thin layer of glue over the back of the grey triangle strip and stick it around the top of the pale grey pot, just beneath its rim. Glue a large tan circle on top of the pot lid to cover the tabs.

Take two of the dark green elliptical pieces and hold one in each hand, so that the folded triangles are at the top and bottom pointing backwards. Gently curve the pieces in your hands and place the semicircles in between each other, slotting together to create whole circles on the front (a). Repeat this process until all six pieces are linked to create a sphere (b).

Take the dark green spiky circles, fold the spikes upwards and glue onto alternate linked circles around the spiky spherical cactus (c).

Apply glue to the tabs folded underneath the cactus and press onto the centre of the lid. To complete the plant, take the two orange flowers, fold the petals upwards, then glue one on top of the other with the petals of the top layer lying between the petals of the bottom layer. Stick the flower in place on top of the cactus.

{06a}

{06b}

{06c}

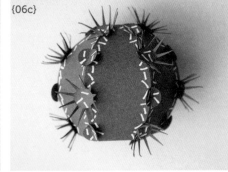

{07} Make the tall, thin cacti
To make the larger of the tall, thin cacti, take the first pale green piece and apply a thin layer of glue over the tab-less half and glue it to the back of the tabbed half of the next piece; repeat to attach the third piece (a). Apply glue to both halves of the final piece (avoiding the tab) and press in place. Repeat to make the smaller version (b).

{07a}

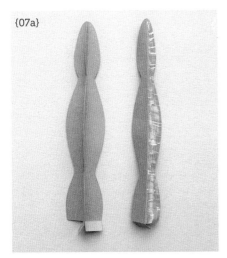

{07b}

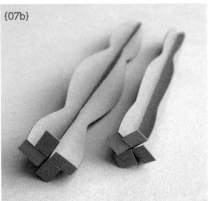

{08} Make the slotted cactus
Start with the two tabbed pieces and slot together so that they stand up to form the base, then slot the other pieces on top. Glue the yellow flowers together (see step 6), then stick in place on the cactus.

{09} 'Plant' the tall, thin cactus and the slotted cactus in the pot
To decorate the final pot plant, spread a thin layer of glue over the back of the pink scalloped strip and glue it around the bottom edge of the dark grey pot. Take the large brown circle and use a pencil to mark out the position of the bottom cross of each of the three cacti. Working on a cutting mat, use a craft knife to cut each cross and slot the tabs of each cactus through. Apply a little glue to each tab and press up to fix them to the underneath of the circle, then glue in place onto the pot lid.

{09}

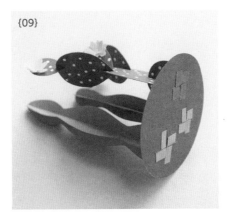

{08}

New to papercrafts?

This section of the book contains all the step-by-step guidance you need to get started. So choose your paper, grab your scissors, and read on to discover all you need to know to become a paper artist!

Seasoned pro?

If you've already completed a few papercraft projects, use this section to build up your skills. Packed with hints, tips and techniques, it will encourage you to explore even more ways to express your creativity, from the simple joys of papier mâché to the skilful arts of quilling and origami.

Techniques

Paper and card

{ *Choosing the right paper or card for your papercraft project is your first and most important step; it can make the difference between a stunning piece and one that is just okay. There is a huge amount of choice available to you, so much so that it can be a bit daunting, so read on to find out a little more before stocking up.*

TYPES OF PAPER

There are two types of paper available for crafters – machine-made or handmade. For each project included in this book, the type and weight of paper used by the project designer is given in the Materials list, but it can be fun to explore the other choices.

MACHINE-MADE PAPER

Even though you may be new to papercrafting, it is surprising just how quickly you can build up your paper stocks. Listed below are some of the types of paper you are likely to come across, although for some techniques, such as origami and quilling, specialist papers are available.

Printed paper: Be prepared to be spoilt for choice. There are so many different patterns available, including incredible faux designs, such as the wood-grain paper used to make one of the loops for the necklace on p. 44. The popularity of scrapbooking (see p. 130) has led to this incredible choice, and you can very easily buy packs of papers in a variety of useful sizes that have been especially selected to coordinate perfectly with each other.

Textured paper: Many machine-made papers are available with textured surfaces. These can be subtle, like the raised dot pattern on the paper selected for the picture on p. 56, and they are a great way to add dimension to your paper work of art.

Tissue paper: This thin, fragile paper is available in an array of beautiful colours and lovely patterns too, but choose carefully as the colour on the cheaper versions may bleed or run.

Crêpe paper: The stuff of children's party streamers, this is tissue paper that has been coated with sizing and run through a process to gather it.

Vellum: This is a strong and durable translucent paper that is particularly good for embossing. In its plain white state it is better known as tracing paper, but you will find that many colours and patterns are available.

Recycled paper: Keep a look out for 'free' paper including newspapers, magazines, catalogues, maps, sheet music, books and wallpaper samples.

HANDMADE PAPER

Handmade paper can be made of different materials and may have inclusions, such as flower petals, grasses, newsprint, plant fibres or metallic flecks. Sometimes the surface can be quite inconsistent due to the handmade process, which is part of the paper's charm. Handmade paper is usually not structurally strong, but can add a whole new decorative dimension to your projects.

Standard paper/cardboard sizes

Metric name	Size in mm	Size in inches
A5	210 x 148	8¼ x 5⅞
A4	297 x 210	11¾ x 8¼
A3	420 x 297	16½ x 11¾
A2	594 x 420	23⅜ x 16½
A1	841 x 594	33⅛ x 23⅜
A0	1189 x 841	46¾ x 33⅛

Note: Every 'A' size is double the previous size. For the metric size in centimetres, move the decimal point one space to the left, so 210mm is 21cm.

Note

In cold, damp weather, paper can become wrinkled, in hot temperatures it may curl and warp, and if left in direct sunlight, the colour will bleach out. Slip your papers between large pieces of card (or an artists' portfolio) and store them flat beneath the sofa.

PAPER WEIGHTS

Paper comes in various thicknesses or 'weights' and weights are measured in grams per square metre (gsm). Here is a general guide.

Lightweight 80–120gsm: The weight of a standard writing paper for example, or a basic photocopier paper (usually 90gsm). Lightweight paper needs to be handled relatively carefully but holds its shape well.

Medium-weight 120–150gsm: This is a very versatile weight of paper. It is strong, yet easy to cut, score, fold and stitch. A good-quality letter paper is about this weight.

Heavyweight 150–250gsm: If working with heavyweight paper, you will need to use a strong glue, and you may find that it is less easy to cut and score, but it will hold its shape well.

tissue paper

origami paper

scrapbooking papers

crêpe paper

metallic paper

TYPES OF CARD

Cardboard is almost invariably machine-made; the surface may be smooth, textured, metallic, matt or glossy, and cardboard can be single-sided (with a good finish on only one side) or double-sided (finished on both surfaces). Gradually build up a stock of different colour sheets of cardboard in a range of the weights you use most often.

CARD WEIGHTS

Card, like paper, is also measured in gsm, and this is a guide to the most common thicknesses available:

150–160gsm: This is very thin cardboard that can be fed through a photocopier, which is useful for printing off templates.

170–180gsm: This denotes a thin and flexible cardboard that folds cleanly, especially when scored.

210–240gsm: A good all-round cardboard weight that keeps its shape. If you require a card heavier than those listed, it is a good idea to use one of the following options as they are easier to cut than some thicker cards with a higher gsm.

Corrugated card: This is a sort of cardboard sandwich with layers of pleated card laid between flat card layers. Corrugated card can have one (single-ply), two (2-ply) or more pleated card layers. It is strong yet flexible and can often be recycled from packaging rather than having to be specially bought.

Single-ply corrugated card.

Foam-core board: This has a lightweight polystyrene core sandwiched between sheets of very thin card. Most often used for exhibition display boards, it is available in a range of different colours and is extremely easy to cut with a craft knife. It is used to make the backing ring for the Autumn garland (p. 30).

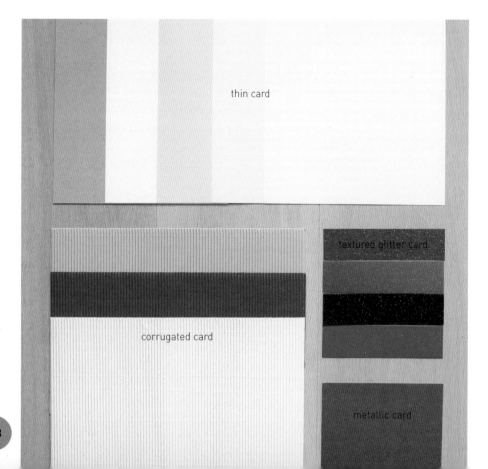

thin card

textured glitter card

corrugated card

metallic card

Tools and materials

The beauty of papercrafting is that you don't need to spend a lot of money on lots of expensive equipment for results that impress. However, there are a few essentials you can't do without – you won't get far without a good range of adhesives and a pair of scissors. Gather together our recommended basic tool kit and put the best of the rest on your birthday list.

Basic tool kit

For most papercraft projects, the equipment listed below may be all you need. It is a good idea to keep all your essentials together in one place, so that you can get started straight away whenever you get the creative urge.

- Scissors
- Craft knife
- Cutting mat
- Metal ruler
- Tracing paper and pencil
- Eraser
- PVA (white) glue
- Glue stick
- Double-sided tape
- Low-tack (masking) tape

ADHESIVES

There are a range of glues and tapes available for applying decorative embellishments and constructing your paper projects. Choose the right one for the job; this will be dependent on the materials being stuck together and the type of project being made. Always check the label for compatibility.

PVA (white) glue: This is a water-based liquid glue that dries clear. It is a good, general-purpose glue suitable for most materials, and diluted with water, it is essential for papier mâché techniques (p. 126).

Glue stick: These tubes of solid glue tend to be less messy than liquid adhesives; simply rub the stick over the area to be adhered to leave an even coat of stickiness.

Glue pen: A liquid adhesive in a handy pen format, ideal for detail work and for sticking small pieces of paper and card with a little more control than a glue stick.

Glue gun: The adhesive is supplied in the form of glue sticks; these are inserted into the gun where they are heated up to release a hot, runny adhesive at the press of the trigger. It provides a strong, fast-tack bond and is useful for working with foam-core board and for sticking plastic to paper.

Superglue: Use this when an instant, long-lasting adhesion is required. A word of caution: it can damage your work surface (and you!) if handled without extreme care.

Spray adhesive: Available in permanent or temporary versions, spray adhesive is ideal for covering large areas, and for fixing delicate items or finely cut motifs (see p. 101).

Double-sided tape: Available in different widths, this is handy for sticking most things.

Low-tack (masking) tape: Useful for holding things in place temporarily without leaving a sticky residue behind. It also makes a good construction tape but needs to be concealed later in the assembling process as it is not very attractive to look at.

Foam mounting pads: Since these have a thickness to them, they are ideal to raise pieces off the surface to give a three-dimensional effect.

Self-adhesive dots: Quick and convenient, these are ideal for keeping glue localised. They generally come in sheets or rolls, but can be expensive.

Note

When applying liquid adhesive, a plastic spreader can help you to achieve an even coating, and a toothpick enables you to apply it to very specific areas.

DOUBLE-SIDED TAPE

This is ideal for attaching larger pieces with straight edges, such as when attaching a panel to the front of a card, for example.

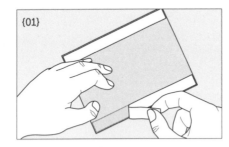

{01}

Apply the tape near the edge of the piece to be stuck and trim the ends within the edges. Peel off a short length of each piece of backing tape and fold back at an angle.

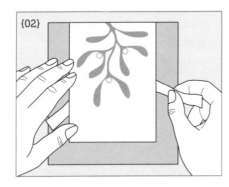

{02}

Position the item, holding the exposed adhesive away from the surface until you are happy with the positioning. Press the exposed area down to hold the item in place, then pull the backing tape tags away and smooth the item down completely.

APPLYING LIQUID ADHESIVE

Lay the item to be stuck face down on a scrap piece of paper – the scrap underneath will allow you to spread the adhesive over the edges so they will adhere firmly. Apply a thin layer of your chosen adhesive to the reverse of the piece to be attached. Be careful not to apply too much as it may be forced out around the edges when the item is pressed into place. Take care not to transfer adhesive from your fingers onto the face of what you are sticking.

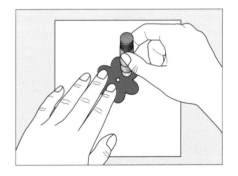

SPRAY ADHESIVE

This is the perfect solution for attaching large or very delicate pieces.

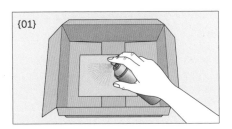

{01}

Spray adhesive is quite messy and it is difficult to control where the spray goes, so place the sheet to be sprayed face down inside a large cardboard box in a well-ventilated area. Shake the can and then spray an even layer of adhesive all over the reverse, holding the can a short distance away from the surface.

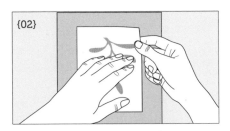

{02}

Position the sheet carefully over the backing material. Smooth it down at one end first, and then smooth your hand carefully over the remaining area, making sure it is firmly stuck down with no wrinkles or air bubbles. If the sheet is not too delicate, you may be able to peel it off and reposition at least once, if necessary.

MEASURING, FOLDING AND CUTTING TOOLS

You may already have many of these tools, but if you do need to purchase them they are widely available in craft stores. You don't need to invest in everything right at the start – make a few projects with what you have already and only buy more equipment as you find you need it.

Plastic ruler: Invest in a good-quality heavy plastic one – the really cheap rulers bend out of shape easily and often do not have accurate markings.
Metal ruler: Can be used for measuring, but mainly for cutting against with a craft knife. Never cut against a plastic ruler because this will quickly damage the edge. A metal safety ruler is best as it has a channel running down its middle to keep your fingers away from sharp blades.
Craft knife: These come in many different sizes, shapes and styles.

For safety, the type with a retractable blade is the best option. For complex paper cut designs, a craft knife with a rotating blade which swivels 360 degrees can enable precision cutting around intricate shapes.
Bone folder: This is used for scoring lines and for creating sharply folded edges as shown in the photo below. The back edge of a table knife makes an acceptable substitute.
Pencils and pencil sharpener: Marks from a soft B grade pencil are easy to remove, but you will need to sharpen your pencil often to keep a fine point.
Eraser: A soft, mouldable rubber can be manipulated into a point for detail erasing and is also ideal for cleaning up backgrounds.
Scissors: Invest in a large pair for cutting paper and card, a small pair for more detailed work, and decorative edge pairs for creating an instant decorative edge.

DECORATING TOOLS AND MATERIALS

There are a whole wealth of decorating tools and embellishing materials that you can buy to make your papercraft projects extra special, from stamps, large and small, to pretty stickers. Here are just some of the options you'll find at any good craft store or website.

Cutting mat: This protects your work surface when cutting. Mats are marked with a grid to help you cut straight edges, and usually have a self-healing surface so old cutting lines do not cause any problems. An A3 size is recommended; the small A4 ones are handy if you want to carry your work with you, but they are likely to prove too small for many projects.

Paper trimmer: This is a useful tool for cutting larger pieces of card. Standard cutting sizes are often marked on the base board, and there will also be a ruler on the cutting guard.

Compass: A useful tool for drawing circles to your exact requirements.

Brayer: A hand-held roller that is useful for rolling over glued paper to be sure everything is stuck down well (see Spraying Over Lace, p. 113).

Embossing tool: A pen-like tool with a metal ball stylus that is used to create a depression in paper when used with a stencil (see Embossing, p. 112), and it also comes in useful for defining scored lines prior to folding.

Awl: A piercing tool for making holes in thick card or to pierce paper ready for stitching, although a large needle also does the job.

Stamps: Rubber stamps are available in an enormous range of sizes, designs and shapes. Alternatively, you can make your own to print a motif or pattern of your own design. Inkpads are generally used to colour-up stamps, but paint or pens can also be used.

Craft punch: Also called hobby punches, these punch out a shape. Again, they are available in a fantastic range of sizes, designs and shapes, and you can build up quite a collection of motifs over time. It can be a good idea to protect your work surface when working with punches and you can invest in a setting mat (a specially durable work mat); alternatively, work on a sheet of thick card.

Border and corner punches: These are a great way to add a decorative pattern to the edge or corners of paper panels.

Single hole punch: A simple hand-held punch, for making single holes of a constant size near the edge of paper or thin cardboard, is particularly useful for making tags.

Stencils: There are many different stencils available for drawing repeated shapes, or you can cut your own designs using stencil card. Lettering stencils are useful for personalising projects, and there are plenty of font sizes and styles available.

Decorative pens and pencils: From the humble felt-tip pen to a gilding pen for adding fine metallic details, there are many options available to you for adding a little extra colour to your finished designs.

Embroidery thread and tapestry yarn: These are great for adding stitched embellishments. Raid your needlework box for pretty ribbons and buttons, too.

Stickers: Adhesive paper stickers are available in an impressive range of designs, colours and finishes. From dome stickers that give a three-dimensional effect to stickers made from interesting textures such as vellum and felt, you'll be spoilt for choice. If you want to add lettering to projects but are not confident in your handwriting, keep a stock of standard sticker messages to hand. Inexpensive stickers are an eye-catching way to seal an envelope.

Decorative brads: An interesting way to attach mounted photo panels and other mementoes to scrapbook pages.

Note

A plastic storage case with drawers is perfect for keeping small embellishment items tidy. Remember, anything decorative can be combined with paper projects, particularly when scrapbooking, so collect attractive pebbles, pieces of wood, shells, buttons and sequins, too.

stencils

rubber stamps

craft punches

stickers

buttons

brads

TRANSFERRING TEMPLATES

Many projects will require images or motifs to be transferred; with a computer and scanner you could use special transfer paper but here is the simplest of methods that doesn't need any special equipment – just a sheet of tracing paper and a pencil.

Note

An HB pencil is best used when tracing as it enables you to achieve a precise line without smudging.

TRACING

It may be necessary to enlarge your project template first, so make sure you keep a look out for any enlargement advice given.

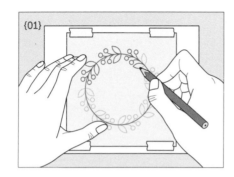

Lay a piece of tracing paper over the motif – if it is large and complex, tape the tracing paper in position with masking tape to stop it moving. Trace the image onto the tracing paper using a sharp, fairly soft pencil.

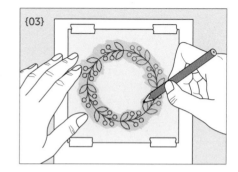

Turn the tracing right-side up again and lay it in position where you want to add the motif. If necessary, tape in place with masking tape. Carefully go over all the lines of the design again, using a sharp pencil.

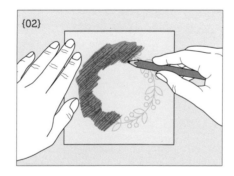

Turn the traced image over and lay it face down on a piece of scrap paper. Shade over the entire image area on the back of the tracing paper, using a soft lead pencil.

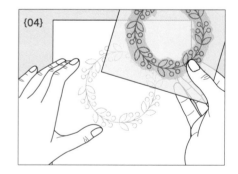

Lift the tracing paper off the base material to reveal the traced image. The transferred pencil lines will usually be quite faint, but if necessary you can go over them again with a pencil or fine pen.

Essential techniques

{ *From identifying paper grain to marking, cutting, scoring and folding card, through to some simple paper-sculpting skills, to help you manipulate a two-dimensional sheet of paper or card into a three-dimensional work of art, you will use the basic techniques covered in this section time and time again.*

WORKING WITH PAPER GRAIN

Machine-made papers are available in many different patterns and textures, yet there is one important characteristic shared by them all.

Machine-made papers have a grain, and working with the grain gives better results. As an experiment, take a sheet of photocopy paper and fold it first lengthways, open it out and fold widthways. Now check the creases; one will look cleaner and sharper – this is the one in the direction of the grain. To establish the grain without creasing: hold the paper by one edge, then try bending the edge at right angles – if it bends more in one direction then that is the direction of the grain.

TORN EDGES

High-quality hand-made papers often have a distinctive deckle edge, and by using the tearing technique illustrated to the right, you will give a similar look to most standard machine-made papers. It can also be used for light- to medium-weight cardboard.

Note the direction of the grain; if the paper is torn across the grain the result can be quite ragged. Lay a steel ruler about 1cm (⅜in) in from the existing edge of the paper. Holding the ruler firmly in place with one hand, tear off the edge of the paper with your other hand, moving your hand down as you work, to tear short sections at a time. If you tear towards yourself it creates a rougher edge. To achieve a smoother, less dramatic deckle-edge effect, tear the paper away from yourself.

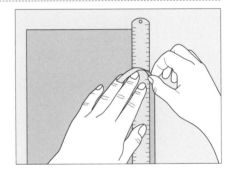

Note

For many projects, you will need to begin with at least two edges straight and at right angles to each other. Use the lines on your cutting mat to check; draw a guideline and trim one edge if necessary. When marking measurements onto paper or card, use light pencil marks so they can be rubbed out easily later.

USING A CRAFT KNIFE

When using a craft knite, don't use a wooden or plastic edge to cut against as it will soon become damaged and will no longer be straight.

CUTTING A STRAIGHT LINE

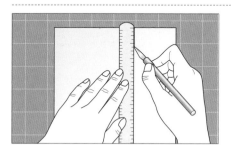

For the cleanest cut, use a steel ruler and a craft knife with a new blade. When cutting, you have the most control when cutting towards yourself. Keep the blade at a 45-degree angle, and press the blade firmly and evenly as you move the knife along the line. Don't press too hard or you may find that the paper wrinkles, giving you an uneven edge. For thicker paper, it may be necessary to draw the blade across more than once: first, draw the blade across without exerting too much pressure, then go again with more pressure to make the final cut.

Note

You can also use a guillotine or paper trimmer to cut straight lines, but test it out on a piece of the same material first to see how it reacts. Hold the paper in position firmly with the other hand to avoid it moving as you cut.

CUTTING A SHAPE

When cutting shaped openings, draw the outline carefully in pencil first. Place the item on a cutting mat and cut around the outline with a sharp craft knife. Keep the blade as vertical as possible while you cut – take your time and try to achieve a smooth shape first time. With practise, a craft knife will give a much smoother line to your cut shape than scissors will.

USING DECORATIVE EDGE SCISSORS

One of the easiest ways to achieve a shaped edge, for a homemade card for example, is to use decorative edge scissors. These are available in many simple designs and here is how to use them.

Cut the pattern close to the original edge of the paper. Open the scissors completely when beginning the cut, but don't close the blades completely at the end of the cut – the last segment of the pattern may not be a perfect repeat. Realign the pattern on the blades carefully with a matching repeat in the cut design, and cut again. Repeat until you have completed the cutting of the whole edge.

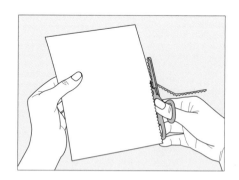

Although you can use a metal ruler when cutting a straight line with a craft knife, it may look even better if you do it by eye, as on the slightly wonky windows of the city skyline on the Foxy nights paper cut (p. 48).

CUTTING FOLDED DESIGNS

Paper-cut decorations that feature folding and cutting paper into symmetrical designs can be made in all shapes and sizes. One of our favourites is the paper snowflake. Fold a simple piece of white paper, make a few snips, then unfold to reveal a beautiful and delicate decoration. And it's easy to make many different designs.

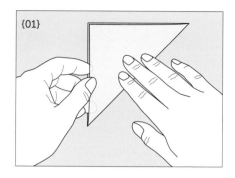

{01}

Cut a piece of either textured or patterned paper to around 10cm (4in) square and fold in half diagonally, to make a triangle. Next, fold the piece of paper in half again down the middle of the triangle, to make a smaller triangle.

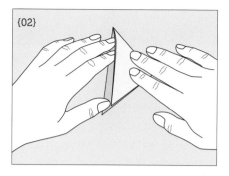

{02}

Next, fold the piece of paper in half again down the middle of the triangle, to make a smaller triangle.

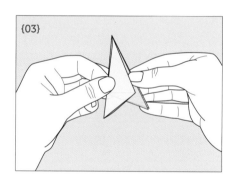

{03}

This time, accordion-fold the triangle into three sections, aligning the long straight edges perfectly each time.

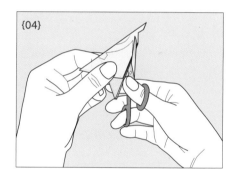

{04}

Draw the outline of part of your snowflake design so it fits onto the folded paper and cut out – experiment with different designs.

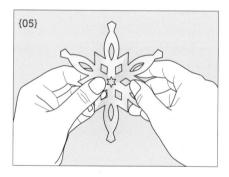

{05}

Unfold the paper carefully to reveal the cut snowflake. Make several more snowflakes in a range of different sizes and shapes.

Note

To remove the folding creases, set an iron to warm, and press each snowflake as gently as possible. A great way of using these snowflakes would be to thread them at random onto several very long lengths of thread, which you could then hang against a wall or a window to create your own paper snowstorm.

SCORING AND FOLDING

Scoring fold lines before you fold thin cardboard or thick paper gives a much neater and crisper fold. Experiment with different scoring techniques on a scrap piece of the material first.

The paper will bend away from the scored line. When score lines are made on both sides of the paper, mountain and valley folds are created, as can be seen on this detail from the star card (p. 9).

SCORING

Place your paper on your cutting mat with the correct side for scoring facing up (note, the scored line will become the inside of your fold). Mark a light pencil guideline with a soft pencil. Place a metal ruler between the marks as a guide and score the line along it by pressing down firmly with the back of the craft-knife blade: you are aiming to break the surface of the paper and care must be taken not to cut right through it. Rub out any pencil marks.

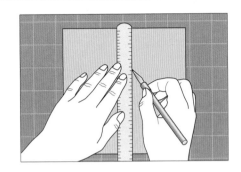

FOLDING

A much crisper fold is achieved when the line is scored first. Fold the cardboard or paper over. For a sharp crease, flatten the fold with the broad side of a bone folder.

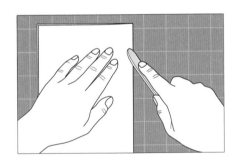

Note
Most materials will fold better with the scored 'valley' on the inside, but vellum folds better with it on the outside.

DOUBLE-FOLD CARD

The design may call for the paper or card to be folded several times – for instance, an aperture card may have an integral backing that folds to the inside. To create a double-fold card, score both lines on the same side then trim 3mm (⅛in) off the outer edge of the right-hand panel, which will fold in to cover the back of the middle panel. The left-hand panel folds the same way to make the back of the card.

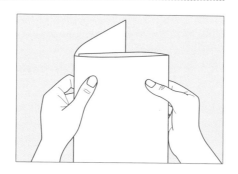

The 3D stag card, p. 11, is made by cutting out three symmetrical shapes, scoring each one along the centre, folding in half and gluing together, back to back.

CONCERTINA FOLDING

For a concertina design, make the first score line on one side of the paper or card and the second score line on the reverse side. Form the concertina by folding one panel forwards and one panel backwards.

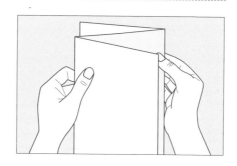

Note

Test folds on a piece of scrap material first if possible, to see how well the techniques work. Materials with loose or obvious fibres, or with inclusions, may not fold very cleanly. Remember, it is easier to fold the paper in the direction of the grain.

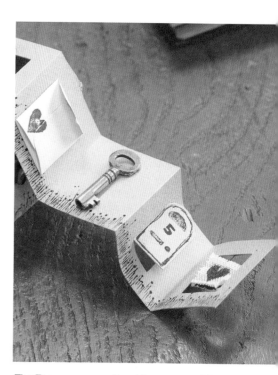

The Teeny-weeny pull-out house on p. 82 is a great way to try out concertina folding.

PAPER MANIPULATION

Papercrafters use many different techniques to sculpt and manipulate two-dimensional paper and card to achieve three-dimensional models.

FRINGING

Draw or score a line near to the top of your strip of paper. This marks the line that you will cut up to and ensures even fringing. Use scissors to snip the paper at regular intervals up to your marked line. To speed up the process, you can fold your strip before cutting.

CURLING

To give shape to thin card or medium-weight paper, roll it gently around a smooth pencil; hold for a few seconds.

Curling the petals makes a very pretty closure for the tops of the Cut and close flower boxes (p. 25).

TABBING

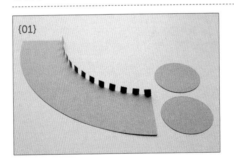

{01}

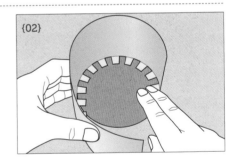

{02}

A strip of paper or card can be manipulated into a curved shape, to make a round box or pot, by cutting tabs along one side. With the wrong side of the paper facing up, mark the border for the tabs along one side of the paper strip, then cut tabs all the way along the border. Turn the paper over and carefully score along the line of tabs. Fold the tabs under to the wrong side.

Curl the tabbed strip between your fingers to make it pliable, then begin to attach the strip to the circle base to form your box/pot. Spread glue onto the folded under (right side) of the tabs and begin to curve the strip around the circle shape, matching up the profile as carefully as you can. Trim the strip to size, overlapping the ends, and press down the tabs onto the circle base with your fingers.

Layers of fringing add to the festive fun on the Mini party piñata (p. 64).

Embellishment techniques

{ There are lots of easy ways to get creative with your papercraft projects, and in this section a few of the most popular are explored. With stencilling and stamping you can decorate plain sheets of paper, and embossing and stitching are great ways to bring textural interest to your paper pieces.

STENCILLING

Stencilling is an easy way to add repeating motifs. You can buy plastic or metal stencils, or make your own. There are many ways to make a stencil, but described here is a simple, straightforward technique that does not need special equipment.

MAKING A STENCIL

If you only plan to use the stencil a few times, make it from thin cardboard, but if you plan to keep it and reuse it many times, make it in acetate instead. Alternatively, invest in special stencil card, which has a waxy coating on one side.

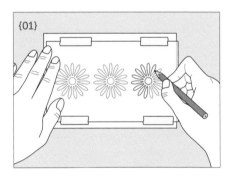

Lay a sheet of tracing paper over your motif and trace it using a sharp pencil. You can use almost anything with a simple shape as a stencil design – but bear in mind that each different part of the design will need to be a separate cut-out.

Transfer the traced motif to a piece of thin cardboard, perhaps arranging several into a larger design. Some motifs may not work well as cut-outs – if so, adapt them at this stage. Cut out the areas to be printed with a sharp craft knife.

USING A STENCIL

Stamping inkpads are ideal for stencilling because they offer strong, semi-dry colour that will not seep under the edges of the cut motif.

Note

To stencil a continuous border, work out the repeat and create alignment marks between repeats that can be removed later. Stencil alternate repeats first, then come back and do the missing ones in between – this will avoid having to place the stencil over wet colour and smudging it.

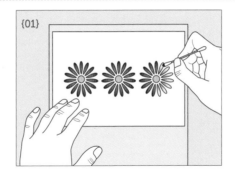

{01}

Position the stencil and hold it firmly in place. Using a sponge, cotton bud or stipple brush, dab colour through the cut-out areas. Use different colours for different parts of the design if you wish; use a clean applicator for each, and allow to dry in-between.

{02}

Carefully remove the stencil, lifting it off directly upwards to avoid smudging the design. Leave the colour to dry thoroughly before adding further details. If the stencil is reusable, clean off the colour as soon as you finish using it.

EMBOSSING

If you have an embossing tool and a light source (ideally a light box), you can use a stencil to create a textured imprint (raised or depressed) onto card. This technique is very often used to bring simple sophistication to wedding stationery. Embossing works both on lettering and on simple motif shapes.

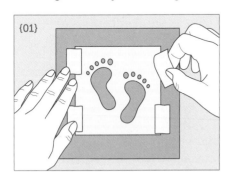

{01}

Place the stencil onto heavy paper or very thin card and secure with low-tack tape. If you apply a little dry soap to the reverse of the motif area the embossing tool will slide more easily.

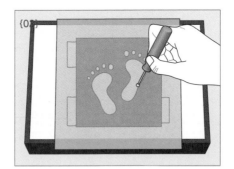

{02}

Turn the cardboard over and place it on a light box, or other light source, so you can see the outline of the design. Using the embossing tool, press gently around the outline.

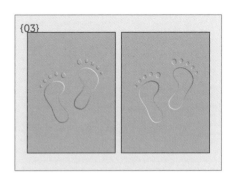

{03}

Embossing from the back gives a raised motif on the front of the card sheet. You can also emboss from the front on some materials, which will give a sunken image.

SPRAYING

Spraying paint is another great way to cover a large area. Many different items can be sprayed over, or you can use a mask so only certain areas receive colour. Use a little spray adhesive to hold the object that you choose to spray over temporarily in place; don't use anything valuable as it will be covered in paint in the end.

SILHOUETTE SPRAYING

Dried botanicals work better than fresh – they are easier to stick down and are already flat, so will give a crisper result.

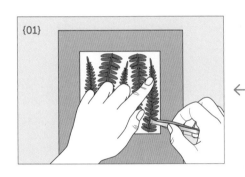

Use a piece of cardboard to mask off large areas that you do not want to colour. Hold the cardboard mask in place securely with a little spray adhesive. Create an arrangement to be silhouetted. When you are happy with the design, stick each item in place with a little spray adhesive. Protect the work surface.

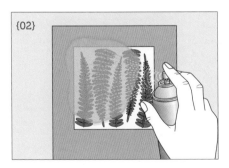

Spray over the entire design in a series of short, light bursts to achieve an even colour. Always follow the directions on the can, and work in a well-ventilated area.

Before the paint is completely dry, carefully peel away the cardboard mask and the sprayed items. It may be easier to lift the edge of each item with the tip of a craft knife first.

SPRAYING OVER LACE

Open-textured fabrics are ideal to create an all-over background design.

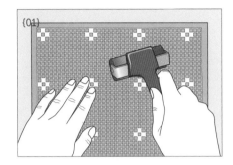

Secure the lace by spraying it on the reverse with spray adhesive, then lay it right-side up over the paper or cardboard. Roll over the fabric with a brayer to make sure it is securely fixed down everywhere.

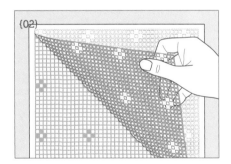

Spray with the paint, as described in step 3 of Silhouette Spraying. Before the paint is completely dry, carefully peel away the lace. Here, the design has been sprayed in white onto a coloured background.

STAMPING

Stamping is ideal to create pattern quickly across large areas, when making giftwrap, for instance. Stamps come in all kinds of designs, but you can also easily make your own.

HOW TO STAMP

Stamping at random is usually very effective, but if you want a regular repeat over a wider area, either lightly mark a grid on the background material or set up a method of aligning the stamp each time so the prints are equally spaced.

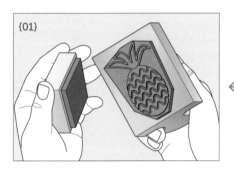

← Apply ink evenly to the stamp with an inkpad. (If the ink is not applied to the stamp evenly, the stamped motif will be uneven in colour.) Smaller stamps can be pressed onto the inkpad directly to load them with colour, but with larger stamps you may need to apply colour by dabbing the inkpad across the surface of the stamp.

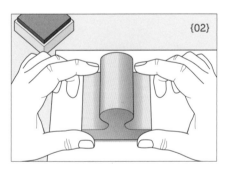

After applying the ink, hold the stamp securely – use two hands if it is a large stamp – and press it down firmly onto the item to be decorated. To avoid a blurred design, don't rock the stamp or move it after it hits the surface.

To avoid smudging, lift the stamp away from the surface cleanly. If the paper or card being stamped is liable to move easily or has a tendency to cling to the wet ink, hold it in position as you remove the stamp.

TWO-COLOUR STAMPING

The two-colour stamping technique described here uses liquid paint; you can also apply each colour with a paintbrush but you will need to work quickly as the first colour may begin to dry. You can also use different colour inkpads but apply each colour separately to the stamp with a clean cotton bud.

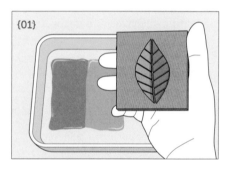

Extra interest can be created when using simple stamp designs by using two colours. Spoon small amounts of each colour into a flat dish and spread out thinly next to one another, to cover an area slightly larger than the stamp. Press the stamp face down into the colours so it is well coated.

{02} Test the stamp on a piece of scrap paper first – the second print after loading up with your ink colour is very often better anyway. Position the stamp and print as normal. To avoid mixing the colours, always press the stamp into the colour the same way around and don't move it around when it is in the colour.

MAKING YOUR OWN STAMPS

Many objects make excellent stamps, so it is worth experimenting with anything you think may be suitable – try shaped cookie cutters, for example. Also, it is easy to make your own small stamps – here are just two simple ideas.

ERASER STAMP

A simple rectangular eraser makes a great base for a stamp. First draw the design on the stamp, but don't make it too detailed because you will need to cut it out. If you prefer, you can work up the design on paper first and then transfer using tracing paper.

A pencil-top eraser makes a good stamp.

Cut around the outline with a sharp craft knife, to a depth of around 3mm (⅛in). Remove the excess material around the motif by cutting into the sides of the eraser, up to the cut outline of the shape. If there are line details within the design – such as the doorway here – you can cut these as a shallow groove.

Apply ink evenly to the stamp as normal and make your stamped print. The finished print will be a mirror image of your original design – this is important to remember if you are working with letters or numbers.

CRAFT PUNCH STAMP

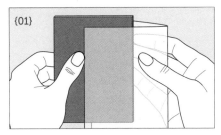

Take a small piece of rubber sheet and wrap a piece of waxed paper around it.

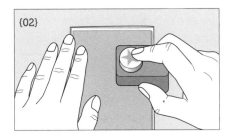

The waxed paper will allow the rubber to slide into the stamp more easily. Punch out your chosen shape from the rubber sheet.

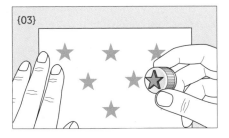

Apply the rubber shape to a mount using a strong adhesive – a plastic bottle cap is perfect for a small motif. For larger designs, use a block of wood. Use to stamp as normal.

PUNCHING

Craft and hobby shops carry a wide range of punches in many designs and sizes. Most are designed to punch paper, but more heavy duty versions will also punch through thinner weights of cardboard.

USING PAPER PUNCHES

{01}

Insert the paper into the punch and press down quite hard – the pressure required depends to some extent on the design and what you are punching through, but some punches are quite stiff. If possible, try before you buy.

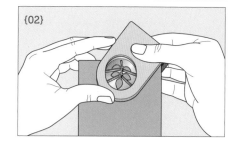

{02}

If the exact position of the punched hole is critical, turn the punch upside down so you can see exactly where the shape will be. Using the punch upside down will also create a mirror image of the motif on one-sided cardboard or paper.

USING A PADDLE PUNCH

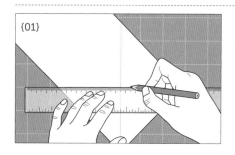

{01}

With this type of punch you can make a hole anywhere on the sheet, so start by marking the position of the hole to be punched lightly in pencil.

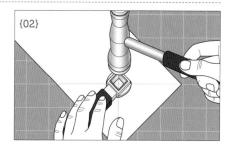

{02}

Place a setting mat on the table to protect it. Centre the punch over the mark, hold it steady and hammer smartly to punch out the hole.

USING A DECORATIVE EDGE PUNCH

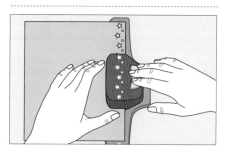

Some punches are specifically designed to create an edge design – they usually have the design repeat shown on either side of the actual punch section, so it is easy to line up the punch for a continuous pattern.

Note

Protect your work surface when using punching or piercing tools. Use an old cutting mat, or better still the special setting mat. Always keep fingers holding the item being punched well out of the way.

STITCHING

Hand-stitching a design is a very effective way of adding both colour and texture to card and heavy paper. It's not ideal for lightweight paper, because this probably won't be sturdy enough to support the thread. Pre-piercing the stitching holes will give a neater result than trying to push a threaded needle through solid paper or card.

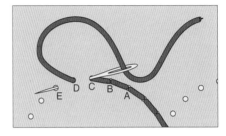

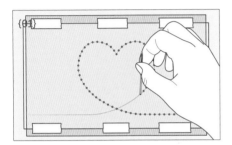

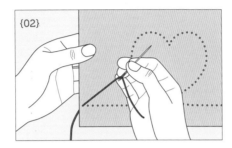

Make a tracing of your chosen design and lay it over the piece of paper or card to be stitched, temporarily attaching it in place with low-tack tape. Choose a suitable embroidery stitch and work out the spacing for the stitch width and the distance between stitches. Use your unthreaded needle to pierce holes through the tracing and onto the paper or card at the stitching points.

Remove the tracing. Thread the needle with a length of embroidery thread long enough to complete the stitching. Knot the end, then bring the needle from back to front through the first hole and pull through until the knot sits against the back surface. Work the design in your chosen embroidery stitch using the pre-pierced holes at all times.

RUNNING STITCH

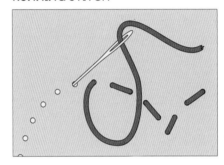

CROSS STITCH

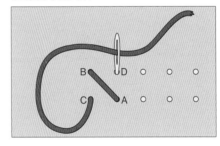

 Even a simple stitch can be a very effective way to add colour and texture.

Note

When you have finished stitching your motif, fasten off the end of the thread on the reverse by looping it round an adjacent stitch and knotting tightly. Trim thread ends neatly.

Origami

{ Origami is a traditional Japanese technique of folding paper into representations of flowers, birds, animals and even little gift containers. Most designs are folded from a simple piece of paper without cutting or adhesive. Explore the common symbols and terms you will encounter in standard origami diagrams.

ORIGAMI MATERIALS

Almost any kind of paper is suitable for origami – although some projects work better with thinner paper, others with thicker, so it is worth experimenting when folding a new design. Special origami paper often has a different colour on each side, which makes folding easier.

CUTTING SQUARES FROM RECTANGLES

Origami paper usually comes in squares, but most other suitable paper comes in rectangular sheets so you will need to cut them down to a square.

CREASING METHOD

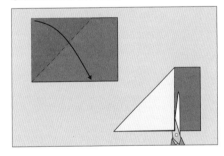

Fold the left-hand edge onto the bottom edge. Hold the edges together and crease firmly all along the diagonal fold line. Holding the bottom point of the triangle firmly, cut upwards with scissors using the vertical side of the triangle as a guide. Unfold the square.

NO-CREASE METHOD

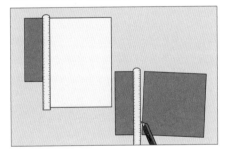

Line up the top and right-hand edge of two identical pieces of paper, one horizontal and one vertical, on a cutting mat. Holding firmly in place, lay a metal ruler along the left-hand edge of the upper sheet. Remove the upper sheet and cut along the right-hand side of the ruler with a craft knife. With a sharp knife, it is possible to cut several sheets at once.

BASIC TECHNIQUES AND FOLDS

Origami diagrams show 'before' and 'after' in sequence, so look ahead to see what the finished fold should look like. All diagrams have written instruction so read these first – it's easy to unfold an incorrect fold, but your design will look better if only folded as necessary.

COMMON ORIGAMI SYMBOLS

In origami diagrams, edges of the paper are shown as solid lines, dash lines indicate folds or creases made in the current step; folds made in a previous step are shown as a narrow solid line. Dotted lines indicate edges hidden behind the model, imaginary lines or the shafts of fold arrows that pass behind the paper.

Transform a sheet of paper into a lovely lily with a few simple folds (p. 16).

  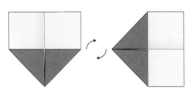

▲ Fold towards you (valley fold). ▲ Fold away from you (mountain fold). ▲ Fold, crease firmly, then unfold. ▲ Rotate 90 degrees.

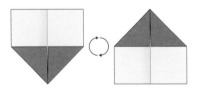    

▲ Rotate 180 degrees. ▲ Turn paper over. ▲ Push here. ▲ Hold here.

REVERSE FOLD

Many of the models use a technique called the reverse fold, in which the end section of the fold is reversed.

◀ Fold over at the point you want the reverse fold to begin. Hold the original fold line just below this point, open out the fold above the point slightly and push down.

◀ The finished reverse fold. Part of the model is now enclosed between two outer layers of paper and a section of the fold now folds the other way.

ORIGAMI SWAN

Make this model to practise your folding skills and your understanding of the common origami symbols. The swan has a long neck, so you will need to begin with a fairly large piece of paper. Use thin paper, as the head requires many tiny folds that will be hard to achieve in thicker paper.

{01}

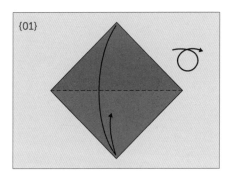

Fold the square of paper in half diagonally, crease firmly and then unfold. Turn the paper over.

{02}

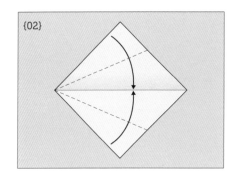

The fold you have just made is now a mountain fold. Fold the top and bottom edges in towards the central crease. Leave a tiny gap between the edges but try to keep the left-hand corner sharp.

{03}

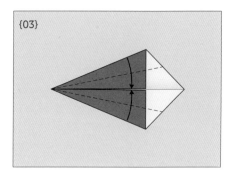

Fold the two outer edges of the new shape in towards the centre crease.

{04}

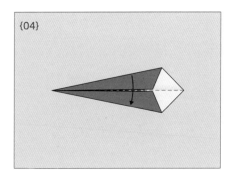

Fold the full shape in half along the central crease – the small gap left in step 3 should mean you can do this without splitting the paper.

{05}

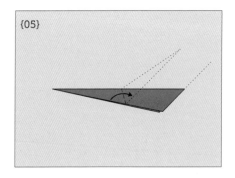

Fold the front point across to the right – there is no location point for this, so do it by eye referring to the diagram. The point should align with the slope of the tail, as indicated by the dotted lines.

{06}

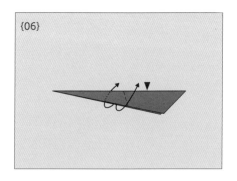

Open out the fold made in the previous step. Push inwards to reverse fold the body into the front point using the creases just made.

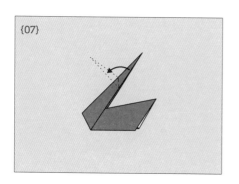

{07}

Continue to form the head and neck by folding over the front point as indicated.

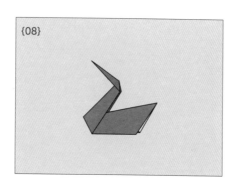

{08}

Open the fold out and make another reverse fold into the front point as before. Crease firmly.

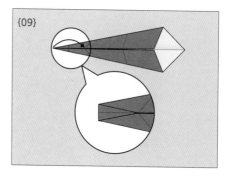

{09}

Open out the reverse folds made in steps 6 and 8 and the fold made in step 4. Fold over the very tip of the front point to the nearest crease to begin forming the beak.

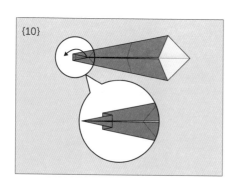

{10}

Fold the tip of the beak back again. Remake the folds from steps 5, 8 and 10.

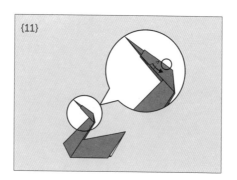

{11}

The head of the swan should now look like this. Refine the shape of the head by making two more tiny folds on either side and reverse fold the front of the head into the neck.

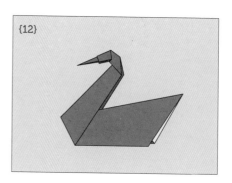

{12}

The finished swan. You could also reverse fold the tail at this point if you prefer.

Quilling

Quilling, or paper filigree as it is sometimes called, is a craft in which strips of paper are rolled, shaped and glued together to create decorative designs. The paper strip is wound around a quilling needle to create a basic coil, which can then be shaped and arranged to form flowers, leaves or ornamental patterns.

QUILLING MATERIALS

Besides the specialist equipment listed here, you will also need small, sharp scissors for trimming ends, and a toothpick or a pair of tweezers for picking up and applying adhesive to small coils. The techniques are simple, if a little fiddly, so you will need a little patience, too.

Coloured paper strips rolled in tight and loose coils will give a modern, graphic look.

Quilling tool: When you first begin quilling you will find it easier if you use a slotted quilling tool that holds the end of the paper firmly as you roll it. This tool does create a slightly larger hole at the centre of the coil, so when you become more skilled you may prefer to simply roll between your fingers or use a needle tool or a toothpick instead.

Quilling paper: Generally, very narrow strips are required to make the quilling shapes. Packs of paper strips are available ready-cut from specialist outlets or good craft stores. As well as a wide range of colours, from pastels to vibrant shades and either plain or shaded in tone, the strips also come in different widths – the 3mm (⅛in) size is the best width for beginners. The strips are normally around 45cm (18in) in length and come packed in a loose figure of eight. Always tear quilling paper to length – don't cut it with scissors or a craft knife because a sharp cut edge will be more noticeable in the finished shape; a soft, torn edge is less visible.

PVA glue: This is the best adhesive to use for quilling as it dries clear – a bottle with a fine tip applicator is ideal.

Quilling board: This will help you to achieve equal-size coils or other shapes for more complex designs.

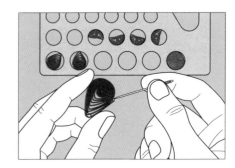

BASIC TECHNIQUES

It couldn't be easier to roll your paper strips into coil and coil variations. You can also squeeze and manipulate your coils into different shapes, which can then be combined to build up an interesting design.

ROLLING THE PAPER

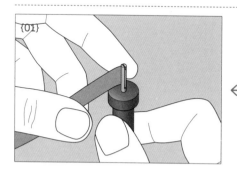

Take half a strip of quilling paper and gently thread one end into the slot in the tool. Make sure that only a very tiny end of paper protrudes on the other side of the slot. Hold the strip between thumb and index finger to keep some tension on the paper as you roll, but don't pull too hard or the paper may tear.

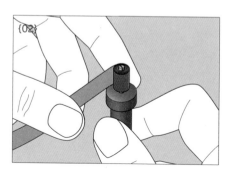

Slowly turn the quilling tool so that the paper winds evenly around the tip, keeping the edges aligned. When using the slotted tool turn the tool to roll the paper, but if using a needle tool roll the paper around the tool, keeping the tool still. When the strip is wound, hold in place for a moment so that the paper remembers its position.

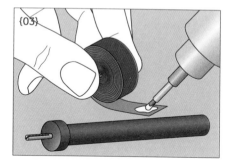

Let go and turn the tool upside down, allowing the quilled coil to fall off onto the table. The paper will begin to uncoil a little; leave it to relax until it stops uncoiling. Place a dab of adhesive on the end of the paper and press gently in place. Hold the paper together for a moment or two until the adhesive dries.

COIL VARIATIONS

TIGHT COIL OR PEG
Wrap the strip around the quilling needle tightly and, before removing it from the tool, stick the end in place with a dab of adhesive. Let the adhesive dry before gently releasing the coil from the tool.

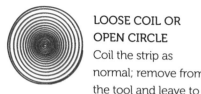

LOOSE COIL OR OPEN CIRCLE
Coil the strip as normal; remove from the tool and leave to relax. Either stick the end down or leave loose. Using open coils can add a light and delicate look to a quilled design.

V-SHAPE
Fold strip in half and roll each end into a coil away from centre crease.

S-SHAPE
Roll the strip from both ends to meet in the middle, starting on opposite sides of the strip.

GLUING AND SHAPING

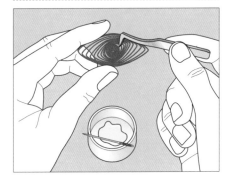

When shaping the coils into other shapes, tweezers are useful to pull the centre of a coil towards the edge to create concentric coils.

This detail from the Quilling shadow box (p. 78) shows just how effective it can be to vary the depth of your coils.

TEARDROP
Pick up a coil with thumb and index finger and gently pinch together at one end, leaving the other end rounded. This is an ideal shape for petals; to refine it, gently press the pointed end towards the centre to create a curve to one side.

TULIP
Make a teardrop shape, but before letting go of the pinched end, push it back towards the centre to create another point on either side. Pinch the two outside points or leave them more rounded.

TRIANGLE
Hold a loose coil between the index fingers of each hand and push the bottom edge up with your thumbs to create the triangle shape. Pinch the three corners but try to keep the centre as round as possible.

MARQUISE OR DIAMOND
Hold the coil on opposite sides between the thumb and index fingers of both hands. Pinch tightly on each side to form points at each end. This shape is one of the most useful in quilling.

CLOSED HEART

Create a triangle, and then push down in the centre of the top side to create the indentation for the heart shape.

SQUARE OR RECTANGLE

Hold the coil between both thumbs and both index fingers and gently press into a square or rectangle shape. Pinch each corner into a point.

CRESCENT

Pinch a loose coil at each end to form points, while pushing in on one side with the tip of a finger or the rounded end of the quilling tool to create a half-moon shape.

LEAF

Make a marquise; after pinching the ends, push both of them in towards the centre to curve them in opposite directions and create a twisted leaf shape.

STAR

Make a marquise, then turn the shape 90 degrees and pinch two more points to make a star. Pinch the tip of each point firmly to sharpen up the shape.

MAKING A PICTURE

Relatively complex quilling designs can be made up using a combination of simple shapes such as triangles, squares, circles or crescents. Select a suitable pre-drawn design template or draw your own design. When creating your own designs, think about how these basic shapes can be put together to create the right effect.

{01} If you are creating a new design, lay a piece of tracing paper over the template and sketch different quilling shapes into different areas to create the shapes. For a flower, there might

→ be one shape for the petals, another for the centres and one for the leaves. Move things around and try substituting variations if necessary, until you are happy with the overall effect.

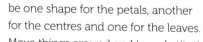

{02}

For a large design, glue small elements together first and then assemble these into the larger design. Use pins pushed into a soft surface – such as thick cardboard or foam-core board – to hold the different parts of each element together if necessary while the glue dries. The finished glued shapes should be very sturdy.

{03}

The finished shape can be placed on a background by putting it in position and then lifting one edge at a time to add a dot of adhesive underneath. Larger shapes can be very flexible and can even be manipulated into three-dimensional shapes. Do not use pins to secure the design to the background at this stage because they will create permanent holes.

Papier mâché

{ The technique of papier mâché is an ideal way to recycle paper into new objects that are both strong yet very lightweight. Whether layered or moulded, papier mâché items need a final layer of decoration, and they can either be painted or a final coat of decorative paper can be applied to finish.

TOOLS AND MATERIALS

As you would expect of a recycling craft, no particular specialist equipment is required. With the main requirements being paper and a bonding adhesive, plus a decorative layer of some sort to finish, the chances are you have most of what you'll need already.

The rounded shape of the letter on this pennant is made by moulding newspaper with tape onto a foam-core board base.

PAPER AND TAPE

Newspaper is an ideal material for papier mâché – it is inexpensive and readily available. Other suitable papers for the foundation include computer printout paper and recycled items such as envelopes, letters or paper bags.

To create a smoother top layer ready for finishing, use tissue paper or paper serviettes. Decorative papers such as giftwrap, tissue paper and crêpe paper can also be used to add final embellishments.

Scissors and a craft knife are useful for trimming edges and general cutting. Masking tape or clear sticky tape will be needed for constructing foundation shapes.

ADHESIVES

Traditionally, papier mâché is made with flour and water paste – a recipe is given for this below. Watered-down PVA (white) glue can also be used.

FLOUR AND WATER PASTE

Mix plain flour into water at a ratio of 1:4 (four parts flour to one part water) to make a thick cream. Dilute with about five times as much boiling water, stirring into the mixture so the paste becomes translucent and thickens. Allow to cool a little and dilute further as required; stir in one tablespoon of salt for every six cups of paste to stop it from hardening too quickly. The paste will keep in the refrigerator for several days.

WATERED-DOWN PVA (WHITE) GLUE

Mix PVA glue and water at a ratio of 1:4 (four parts glue to one part water).

MOULDS AND ARMATURES

Many items can be used as moulds – bowls, plates, cups – depending on the final shape required and which papier mâché technique you are using. Lubricate the mould with a release agent, such as petroleum jelly, so the papier mâché can be removed easily. Alternatively, cover the mould in cling film, although this may leave crinkle marks on the final object.

To make a framework base for the papier mâché – known as an armature – plastic-coated garden wire is ideal; it is flexible and the plastic coating will protect the wire from the moisture in the adhesive so it will not rust. For bulkier shapes, wire netting can be cut and bent into many different forms and then covered with papier mâché. Some shapes can be built up on cardboard or on plastic containers or even over an inflated balloon – consider the final shape required when choosing what to use.

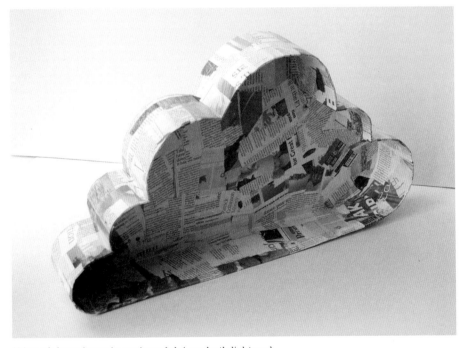

Although large items in papier mâché are both light and strong, the starting base will need to support the weight of the wet paper, which can be quite heavy until it dries. So to make the cloud shelf (p. 34), a sturdy 2-ply corrugated card was used for the back board.

FINISHING MATERIALS

Fine sandpaper can be used to smooth rough edges before the final finish is applied – smooth the surface as much as possible first by adding a couple of layers of a fine paper, such as tissue.

As an initial inexpensive undercoat – particularly if the base is made of a printed paper such as newsprint – ordinary white household emulsion paint is perfect. Acrylic paints are ideal to colour the finished item; they are mixable with water while working, but dry to a silky, waterproof finish and are available in a wide range of colours.

Apply at least two top coats of a suitable varnish to seal the surface – but do not use a water-based varnish on top of water-based paint or the colours will smear.

Once the papier mâché layers have thoroughly dried out, you can decorate your finished model. For the cloud shelf, acrylic paints were used to paint the exterior white and the interior bright.

BASIC TECHNIQUES

There are two basic papier mâché techniques: layering and moulding. Papier mâché can also be made by shaping paper pulp, either in a mould or sculpting with it like clay. Allow the papier mâché to dry completely before beginning to decorate.

LAYERING

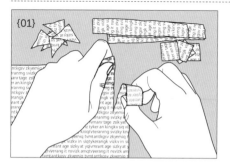

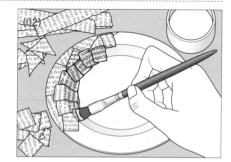

The simplest papier mâché technique is layering, in which pieces of paper are torn into strips, squares and triangles. The pieces are torn and not cut, because rough uneven edges blend together more smoothly than regular straight edges will.

Paste the pieces over a mould and allow to dry. Remove the mould, leaving a hard papier mâché shell. Alternatively, cover a framework of the basic shape – in this case, the framework remains in place under the paper (see the cloud shelf, p. 127.)

For the Wise owl bowl (p. 12) paper was layered over an inflated balloon.

Note
Use different colours for alternate layers or layer the paper in a different direction so it will be easy to see when you have completed a layer.

MOULDING

Soak torn-up newspaper in water overnight. Drain, then boil in clean water for 30 minutes, until the fibres begin to break up. Whisk the pulp in batches in an old food processor or blender. Sieve the pulp, squeezing out the excess water.

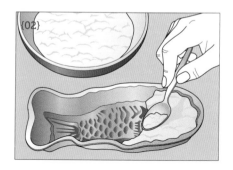

When you have enough pulp, mix in the adhesive to form a clay-like consistency. Mix ready-made dry paper pulp with water, following the directions on the bag. Press the finished pulp into a mould, or use it to build up a shape as you would with clay. If the finished papier mâché is hard to remove from the mould, you can gently loosen it away from the sides with a palette knife.

MAKING ARMATURES

Although it is possible to build up many shapes just using papier mâché, it can be easier and quicker to create a basic framework to work on. To save time, always start with a base of about the correct size and shape.

The blue tit (p. 85) is built up on a wire frame.

ANIMALS AND FIGURES

Plastic-coated wire is best for the armature because it is easily available, inexpensive and will not rust when the papier mâché is applied.

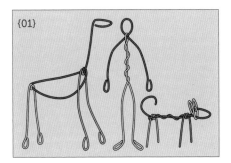

{01}

Bend lengths of wire and twist together securely to form the shapes. The different lengths used to make up these figures are shown here in different colours for clarity.

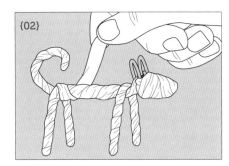

{02}

To start rounding out the basic shape, wrap the wire framework with fairly large pasted strips to create a bulkier outline where required. Add further detail in selected areas using smaller pieces of paper.

HANDLES AND SPOUTS

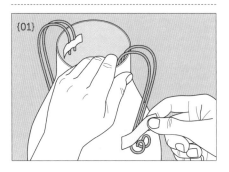

{01}

For handles, create the basic shape in wire and tape to the side of your papier mâché bowl or vase. Cover in papier mâché as normal.

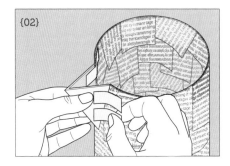

{02}

To make a spout, cut a triangular piece out of the top edge of the main shape. Cut a larger triangle of cardboard, fold in half and then open out. Tape this triangle securely over the cut-away triangle to form the spout.

BUILDING UP FLAT SHAPES

Cut the main shape from thick cardboard. If you want to add narrow pieces protruding from this, support them underneath with toothpicks or short lengths of wire, and tape everything in place using masking tape. Mould papier mâché pulp on top to create the desired shape.

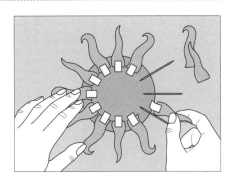

Scrapbooking

{ *Scrapbooks are collections of memories in a visual form, with the selection, arrangement and embellishing of photos into albums. Sometimes known as journaling, it is a very personal craft to be shared with family and friends. It's all about planning – selecting your papers, embellishments and photos to tell your stories.*

TOOLS AND MATERIALS

Many standard papers and other materials contain chemicals that may damage photos, or which can be unstable so they fade or discolour. Look for scrapbook-friendly products marked 'acid-free', 'PVC-free', 'lignin-free' or 'archival quality'.

Paper: The choice is overwhelming and they can be bought in sizes to fit scrapbook album sizes, the most common being 30 x 30cm (12 x 12in) and 15 x 15cm (6 x 6in).
Scrapbooks: These are really just photo albums. There are many different types of ready-made scrapbooks available, some with fixed pages and others of the ring binder type, to which you can add plastic sleeves to hold your pages.

Cutting templates and cutter: These are useful tools for cropping photos into different shapes and sizes.
Fixings: There are many different ways to fix photos and other memorabilia to your pages, from self-adhesive photo corners in every conceivable colour

to specially made pockets, ideal to accommodate items that are designed to be removed. Top of our list are brads. A brad is really just a fancy paper fastener that provides a simple adhesive-free way to fix things in place on the page.

Brads come in many guises from flowers to fancy gems.

PRESENTING PHOTOGRAPHS

Most scrapbook pages will incorporate photographs, and how you choose and present your photos will determine the overall success of your finished page.

CROPPING PHOTOGRAPHS

Cropping can transform a poorly composed or boring picture into a stronger image by focussing the eye. L-crops allow you to try different versions of the crop before beginning to trim or frame the image. They are usually made from black cardboard, but a neutral grey will also work well.

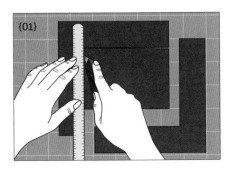

Draw two L-shape right angles on a piece of thin black or neutral grey cardboard, with each arm 5cm (2in) wide and at least 15cm (6in) long. Cut the two L-shapes out.

Carefully mark one corner of the crop on the framed image and measure from here, noting the measurements down. Remove the L-crops and trim the picture to size.

$\rightarrow$

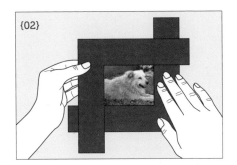

To decide on a crop, place the two L-crops over the image and slide them around to focus on different areas of the picture. Be bold – unusual crops can be very effective.

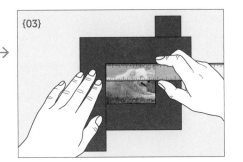

SINGLE MATTING

Single matting gives a single contrast border to help your photos stand out.

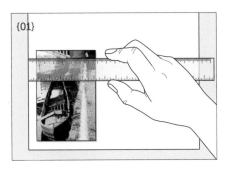

Lay the photo on a large piece of thin card, positioning it near a corner; move it in and out to try different border widths. When you are decided, measure the border, multiply by two and add the width of the photo, then repeat for the height if it is not square.

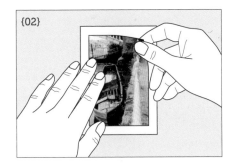

Cut the card to size. Stick the photo down centrally on top of the mat; you can make tiny pencil positioning marks on the mat before placing the photo.

MULTI MATTING

Multi matting gives two or more borders to ensure your photos don't become lost against the background.

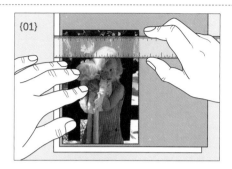

{01}

Lay two or more pieces of card down with the photo on top, so one corner of all layers is visible. Adjust the width of the border on each layer until you are happy with the effect.

{02}

Measure and cut each mat following the steps for Single Matting, p. 131. Stick the photo onto the top mat and then stick the matted photo onto the next layer – and so on if there are more than two layers.

PHOTO MOSAIC

Several similar photos can be combined to make a bigger image for more dramatic impact. This type of mosaic works best when two related images are used – here, two different views of the sea have been combined. When choosing the photos to use, pick examples with similar colours and a similar tonal scale.

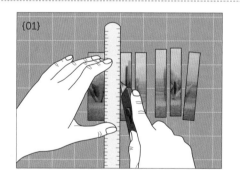

{01}

Stick lengths of double-sided tape over the back of the photo that will form the background mosaic, but do not remove the backing yet. Turn the photo over and cut it into strips for the mosaic, which can be even sizes or in different widths and lengths.

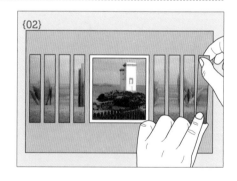

{02}

Single mat the main image and stick it in position on the page. Remove the backing on the mosaic strips and stick them on either side, keeping them evenly spaced. If there is a strong horizontal line, such as a horizon, try to keep it fairly level for the best effect.

CREATING TEXT

Almost all scrapbook pages will have some form of text, even if it is only a title, a motto or a caption. Neat handwriting is perfectly acceptable, but if you are not confident about achieving a good result there are many other options available to you. Here are just a few.

LETTER STICKERS

Before removing the backing, arrange the stickers in a straight line where they are to go, using a ruler as a guide. Peel off the backing and stick the letters down one by one. For a more random, casual look, arrange the letters by eye on the page at slightly differing levels.

RUB-DOWN LETTERING

Rub-down lettering can be applied directly to the background of a project and is available in alphabets and as ready-made words or mottoes. Choose what you want to transfer, peel away the protective backing and rub down on the front of the carrier sheet following the manufacturer's instructions.

COMPUTER-PRINTED LETTERING

Using a computer to generate titles and text offers endless opportunities, particularly with a colour printer. A computer with a reasonable quality printer will produce attractive-looking and grammatically correct text quickly and easily. You can play around onscreen before printing, trying different fonts, sizes and colours – and often arrange text in circles or other shapes with the click of a mouse.

LETTER STAMPS

To print in a straight line, make up the word with the individual letters and push the faces against a steel ruler to make sure all the letters are sitting level. Move the ruler away carefully without moving the letters and lay a strip of masking tape along the side of the letter handles. Wrap the tape right around the handles to keep the letters together in a block as you stamp.

Note

Use the block to stamp the word in position on the paper. To add extra interest you could try using different colours for different words or to highlight one word to make it stand out more. If you are stamping several lines, draw light guidelines in pencil.

FOUND LETTERS

Letters torn or cut from magazines and made up into words using a collage technique can also be very effective. Carefully tear or cut out the letters you need and stick each letter down individually, using paper adhesive. You can either stick them direct to the page, or onto another sheet of paper that you then apply to the page.

Number stickers are a good way to add a date to your page.

TEMPLATES

Use actual size unless otherwise specified.
Visit www.pavilioncraft.co.uk for full-size
templates ready to download

Bow

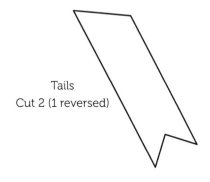

Tails
Cut 2 (1 reversed)

Star

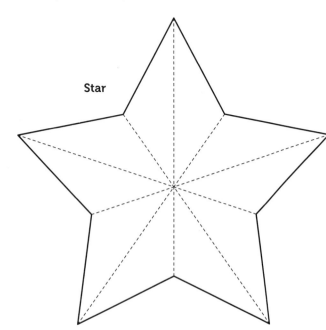

Score and fold along dotted lines

Heart

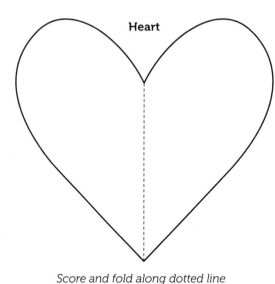

Score and fold along dotted line

Apple

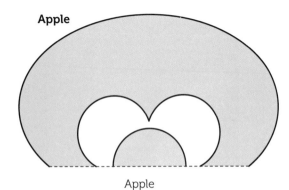

Apple
*Cut along solid lines; score and
fold along dotted line*

Stalk

Bow
*Score and fold along
dotted lines*

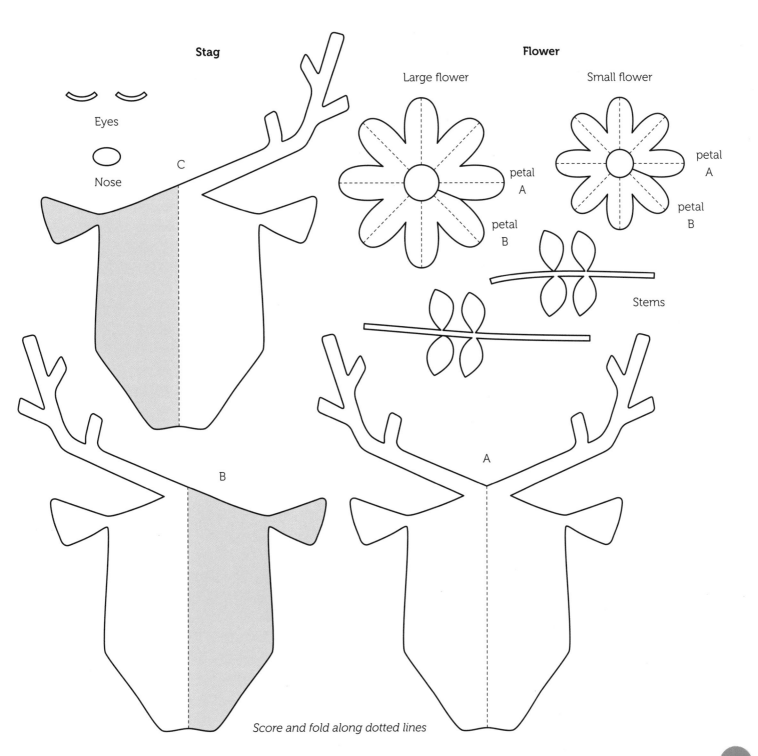

Stag

Flower

Large flower

Small flower

Eyes

Nose

petal A

petal B

petal A

petal B

C

B

A

Stems

Score and fold along dotted lines

CUT AND CLOSE FLOWER BOXES

Score and mountain fold along dotted lines

Square box   *Enlarge by 200%*

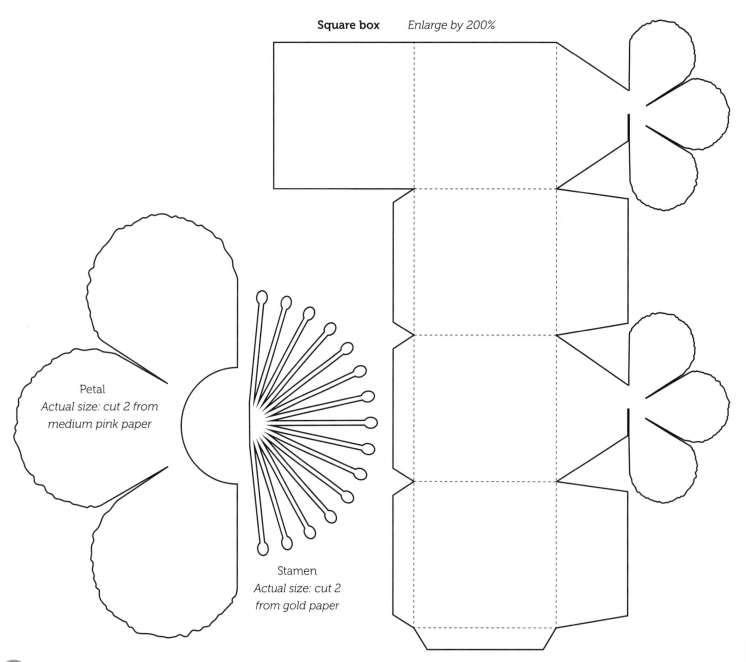

Petal
*Actual size: cut 2 from
medium pink paper*

Stamen
*Actual size: cut 2
from gold paper*

Mollie MAKES HOW TO CRAFT WITH PAPER

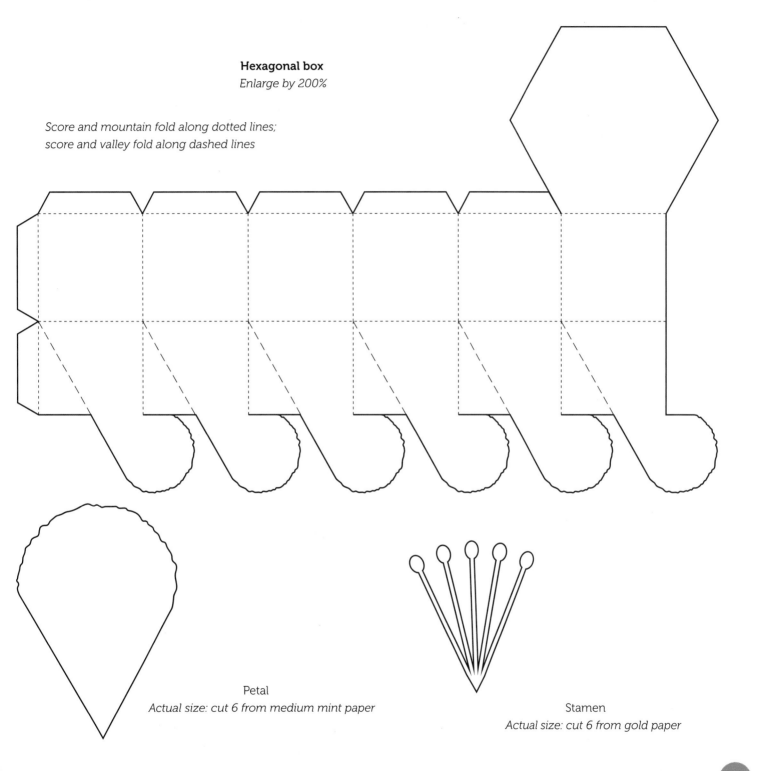

Hexagonal box
Enlarge by 200%

Score and mountain fold along dotted lines;
score and valley fold along dashed lines

Petal
Actual size: cut 6 from medium mint paper

Stamen
Actual size: cut 6 from gold paper

WISE OWL BOWLS

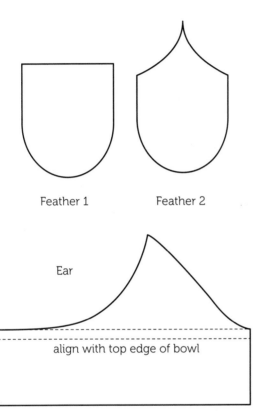

Feather 1   Feather 2

Ear

align with top edge of bowl

SEW PRETTY LOOP NECKLACE

Loop

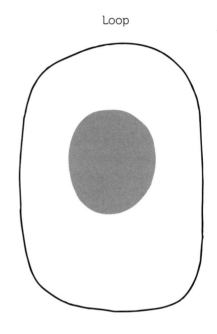

Cut out shaded area

STITCHED PHOTO NAPKIN RINGS

Heart embroidery motif

AUTUMN GARLAND

Leaves

Pumpkin stalk

Small flower

Large flower

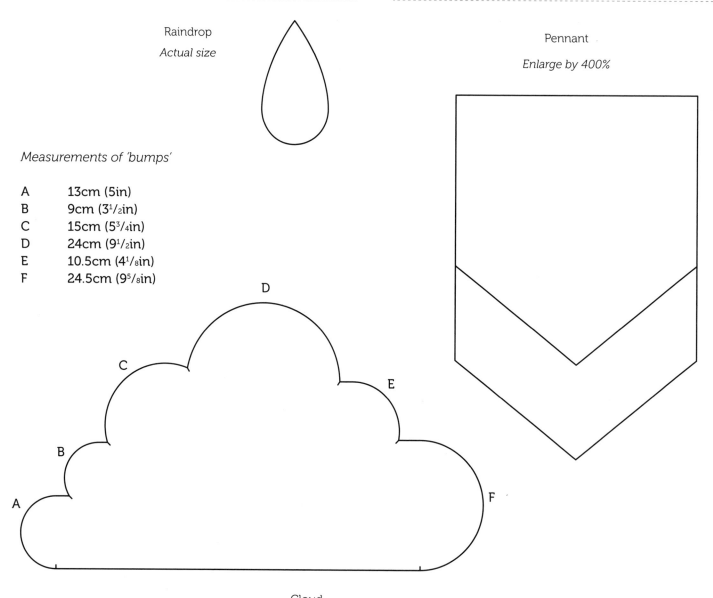

PAPIER MÂCHÉ CLOUD SHELF

CAPITAL LETTER PENNANT

Raindrop
Actual size

Pennant
Enlarge by 400%

Measurements of 'bumps'

A   13cm (5in)
B   9cm (3$\frac{1}{2}$in)
C   15cm (5$\frac{3}{4}$in)
D   24cm (9$\frac{1}{2}$in)
E   10.5cm (4$\frac{1}{8}$in)
F   24.5cm (9$\frac{5}{8}$in)

D

C

E

B

A

F

Cloud
Enlarge by 400%

Kissing foxes

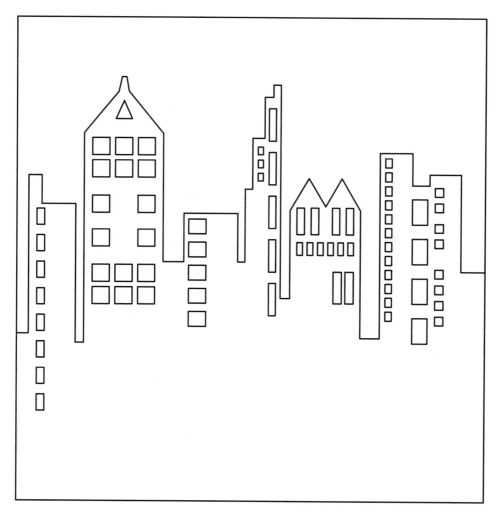

City skyline

Night sky

Teepee
Enlarge by 200%

Score and mountain fold along dotted lines; score and valley fold along dashed lines

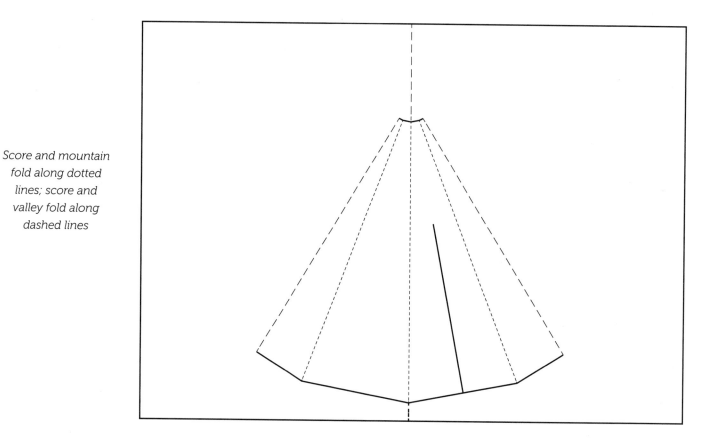

Teepee base

Enlarge by 200%

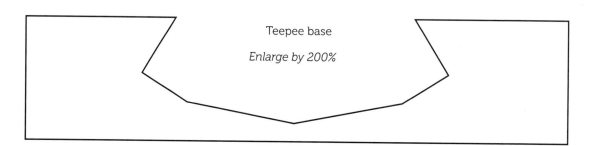

Teepee decoration

Actual size: Cut 1 of each unless otherwise specified.

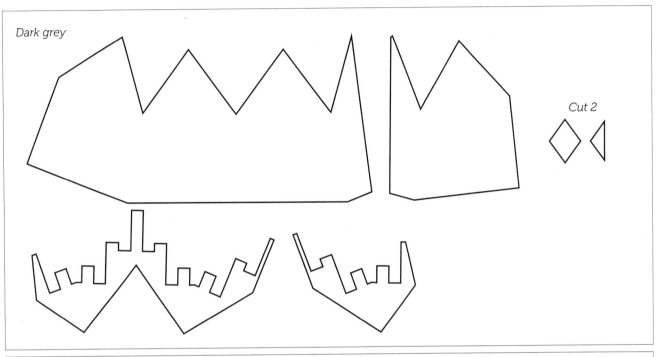

Dark grey

Cut 2

MInt green

Cut 4

Teepee decoration

Actual size: Cut 1 of each unless otherwise specified.

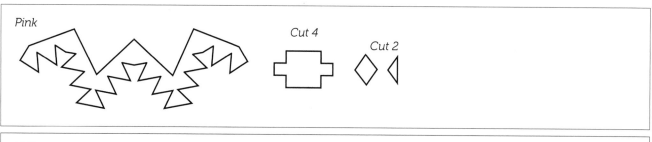

Pink

Cut 4

Cut 2

Yellow

Cut 4

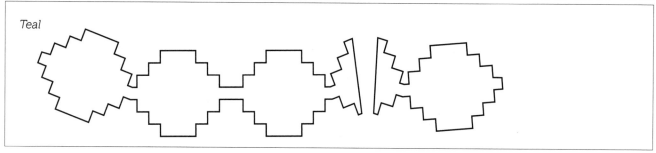

Teal

Front of card decoration

Actual size: Cut 1 of each unless otherwise specified.

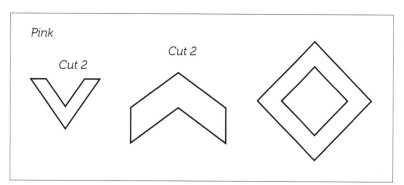

Pink

Cut 2

Cut 2

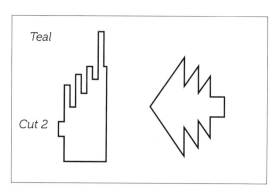

Teal

Cut 2

Front of card decoration

Actual size: Cut 1 of each unless otherwise specified.

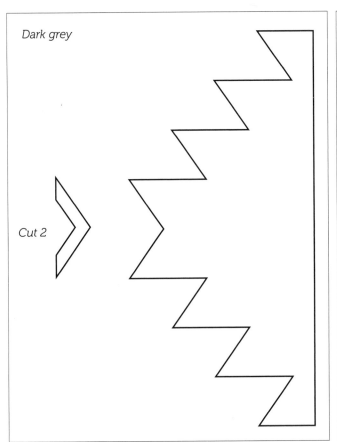

Dark grey

Cut 2

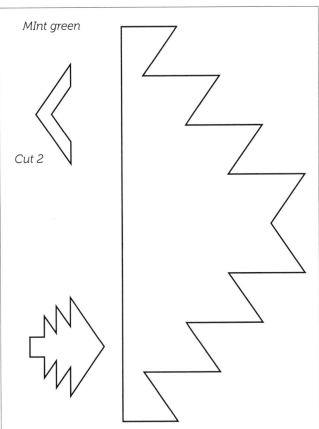

MInt green

Cut 2

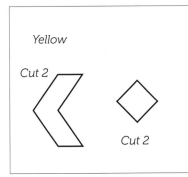

Yellow

Cut 2

Cut 2

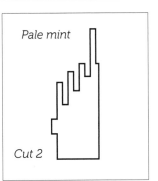

Pale mint

Cut 2

TEENY-WEENY PULL-OUT HOUSE

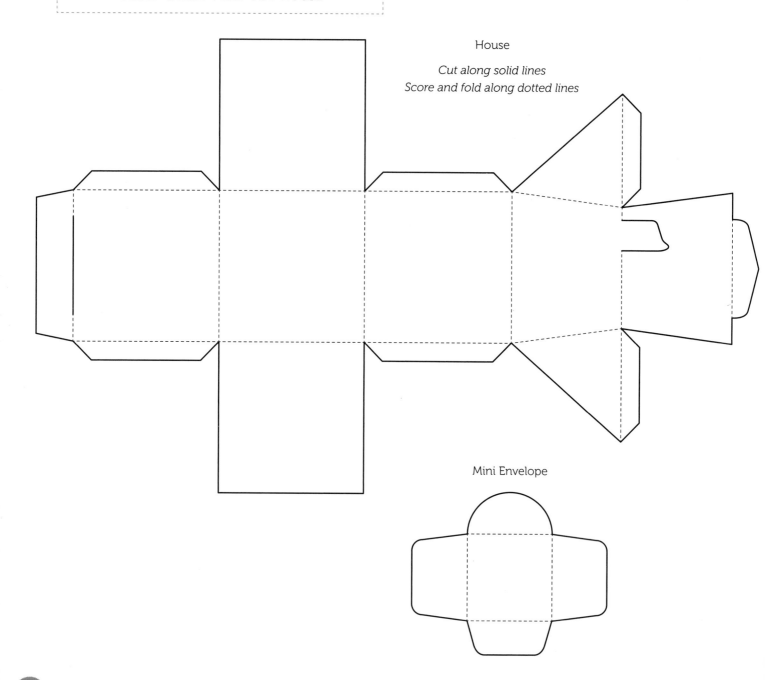

House

Cut along solid lines
Score and fold along dotted lines

Mini Envelope

Mollie MAKES HOW TO CRAFT WITH PAPER

Whiskers

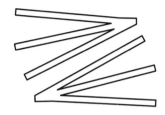

Arms

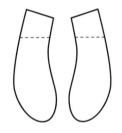

Rabbit

Squirrel

Back

Front

Acorn

Mollie MAKES HOW TO CRAFT WITH PAPER

Owl

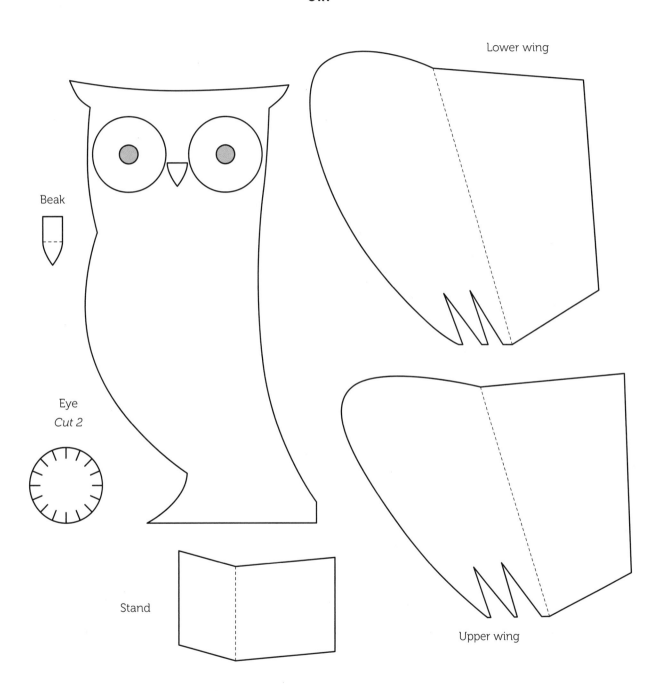

Lower wing

Beak

Eye
Cut 2

Upper wing

Stand

MINI PARTY PIÑATA

Seed

Cut 10

Pull tab

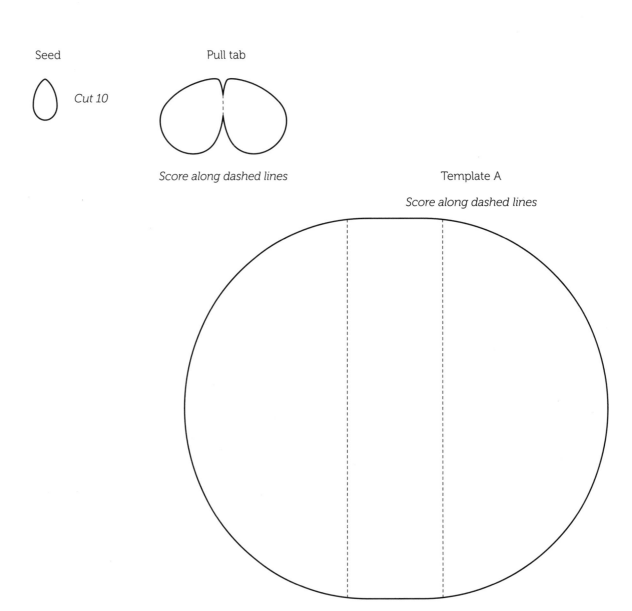

Score along dashed lines

Template A

Score along dashed lines

Mollie MAKES HOW TO CRAFT WITH PAPER

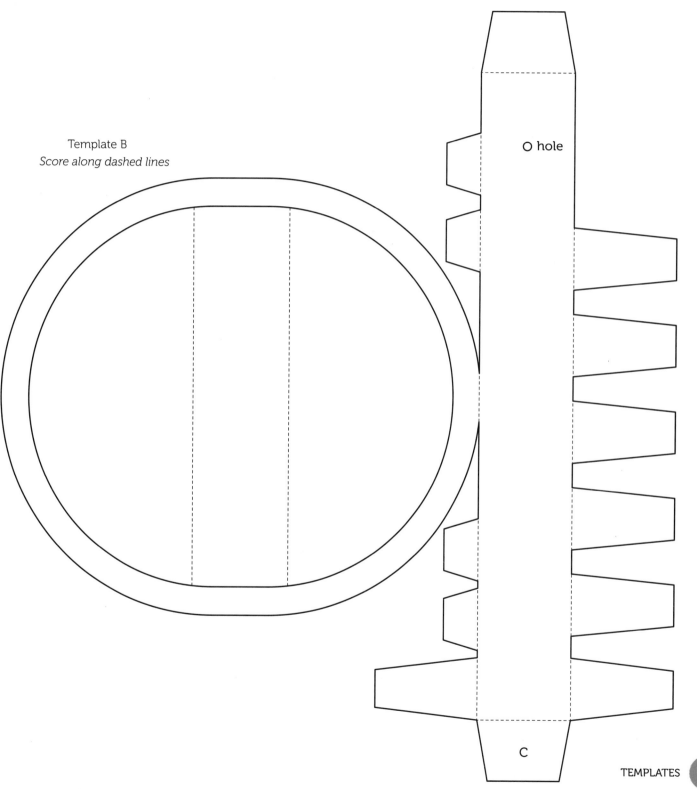

Template B
Score along dashed lines

O hole

C

QUILLING SHADOW BOX

Front frame
Enlarge by 200%

Box frame base
Enlarge by 200%

Cut along solid lines; score
and fold along dashed lines

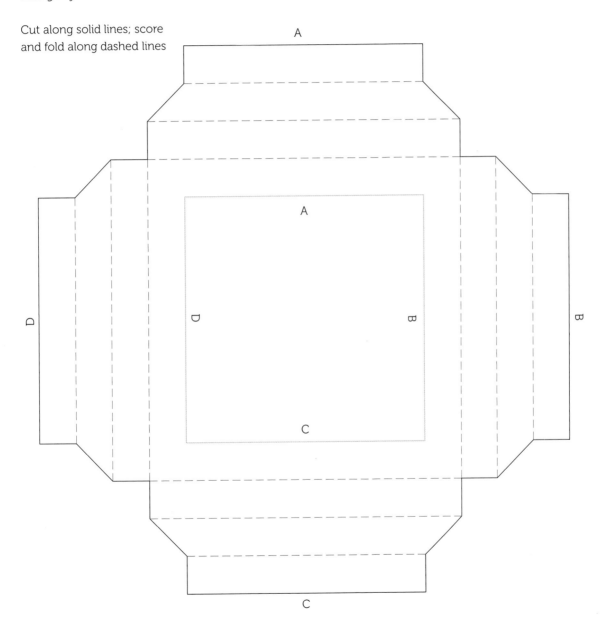

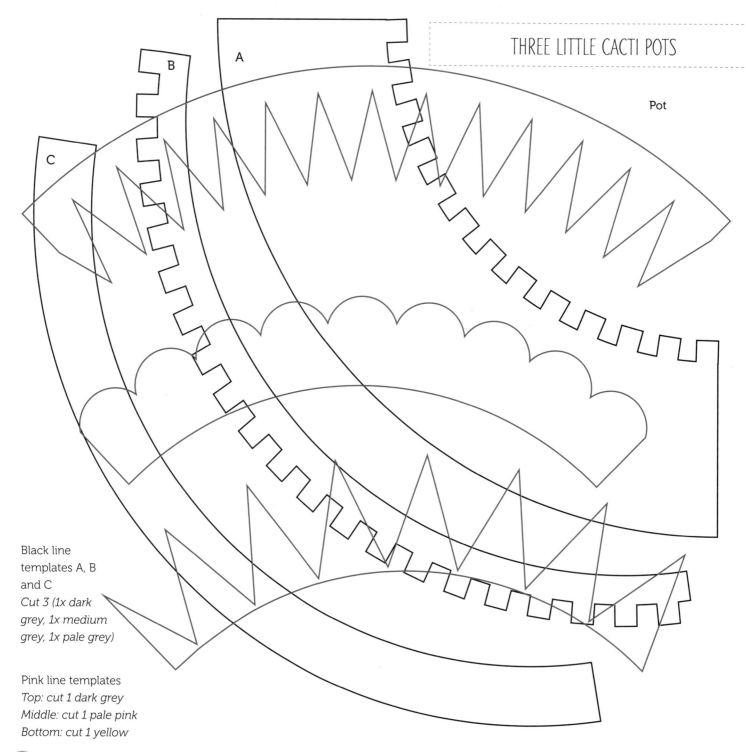

THREE LITTLE CACTI POTS

Pot

B

A

C

Black line
templates A, B
and C
*Cut 3 (1x dark
grey, 1x medium
grey, 1x pale grey)*

Pink line templates
Top: cut 1 dark grey
Middle: cut 1 pale pink
Bottom: cut 1 yellow

Pot continued

Large circle
Cut 1 dark grey, 1 medium grey, 1 pale grey, 1 brown and 2 tan

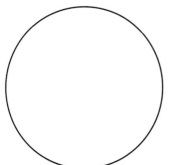

Small circle
Cut 2 dark grey, 2 medium grey, 2 pale grey

Score and mountain fold along dotted lines; score and valley fold along dashed lines

Spiky spherical cactus

Cut 6 dark green

Tall, thin cacti

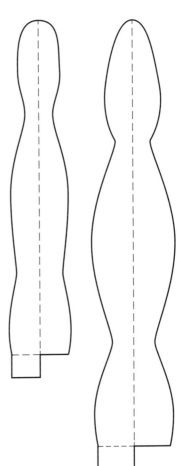

Cut 4 pale green

Cut 2 orange

Cut 12 dark green

Cut 6 yellow

Succulent

Cut 1 of each pale green

Slotted cactus

Cut 1 of each dark green

Score and mountain fold along dotted lines; score and valley fold along dashed lines

INDEX

For more information
on Mollie Makes
please visit
www.molliemakes.com

PUBLISHER'S ACKNOWLEDGEMENTS

This book would not have been possible without the input of all our fantastic crafty contributors. We would also like to thank Cheryl Brown, who has done a great job of pulling everything together and Sophie Yamamoto for her design work. Thanks to Kuo Kang Chen for his excellent illustrations, and Holly Jolliffe for her photography. And of course, thanks must go to the fantastic team at Mollie Makes for all their help, in particular Lara Watson, Helena Tracey and Kerry Lawrence.

PAVILION

Whatever the craft, we have the book for you – just head straight to Pavilion's crafty headquarters.

Pavilioncraft.co.uk is the one-stop destination for all our fabulous craft books. Sign up for our regular newsletters and follow us on social media to receive updates on new books, competitions and interviews with our bestselling authors.

We look forward to meeting you!

www.pavilioncraft.co.uk

Published in the United Kingdom in 2017 by
Pavilion
43 Great Ormond Street
London
WC1N 3HZ

978-1-911216-67-4

A CIP catalogue record for this book is available from the British Library.

10 9 8 7 6 5 4 3 2 1

Reproduction by Mission Productions Ltd, Hong Kong
Printed and bound by 1010 Printing International Ltd, China

This book can be ordered direct from the publisher at www.pavilionbooks.com

Photography by Holly Jolliffe
Illustrations by Kuo Kang Chen